THE

Parsons College

BUBBLE

THE
Parsons College
BUBBLE

A TALE OF
Higher Education
in America

BY

JAMES D. KOERNER

Basic Books, Inc., Publishers

NEW YORK : LONDON

Foreword

BY JACQUES BARZUN

If the saga of Parsons College were not attested fact, it would be necessary to invent it. Every American citizen who is concerned with "trouble in the universities"—not excepting the academic citizen who has the trouble on his doorstep but thinks himself free of Parsons' complaint—must take in and ponder the events described in these pages. And he must not believe for a moment that that tragicomedy was something which occurred at Fairfield, Iowa, and which is now over.

The story of Parsons is an image, only slightly magnified, of what has overtaken American higher education during the last quarter century, and has brought it to a state of moral, financial, and administrative bankruptcy. The magnification inherent in the causes and effects at Parsons is what makes Dr. Koerner's brilliant and deadly recital not *a* document, but *the* document of highest importance to the academy and to the nation at the present time.

The principle at work in the educational debacle we are witnessing is the ancient one of *corruptio optimi pessima*— the corruption of what is best turns out the worst; the fallen angel is the deepest-dyed sinner. And as usually happens, it is out of the best motives that the worst errors come. So it was in the present case. The fundamental cause of the corruption of higher learning has been the desire of college and university to "serve the community" in a direct, visible, measurable way, and earn the rewards of "service."

The first false step was to assume that *study* was not enough to justify an educational institution; that is, study by the young at the feet of masters who also studied to increase knowledge. No, that knowledge, it was decided, must be applied and shown off. The university must make sorties outside the walls. The teacher must leave his post and begin to serve—the city, business, government, foreign states. These services were well remunerated, on top of the continuing salary for the work neglected inside the walls—teaching. Everybody saw and deplored the "flight from teaching," but nobody shot down the pigeons. On the contrary, on campus and off, the range and extent of public service were recorded and envied, boasted about and advertised to potential donors and the community at large.

Soon there was a shortage of academic personnel, and competition between institutions for the "great men" who were performing the new, true service dealt the last blow to learned humility, calm thought, and ethical behavior. The new man in academic life now lusted explicitly after money, after prestige, and after conditions of work that eliminated teaching and substituted expense-account travel on missions. True, only a minority got the chance, but that minority set the pace, earned the plaudits, became accepted as the mainstay and justification of the American university.

Meanwhile the influx of the new generations and the inflating cost of living confronted administrators with insoluble problems. They must take in more students, each one representing a loss (since the market keeps tuition well below costs); they must put up new buildings; they must compete for expensive professors contributing only homeopathic amounts to teaching; they must spend money recruiting the best students for prestige; they must beg foundations for project money for prestige; they must seek government contracts for prestige; and they must widely puff and advertise this whole swoosh, in order to be able to launch fund-raising campaigns.

During and after campaigns, foundations and fund donors

poured in money on the basis of all this service to the city, the nation, and the world, and naturally enough sought to increase the return in kind by promoting a never-ending series of fresh, indispensable projects, institutes, centers—in a word, special arrangements for draining off talent into the busy world.

This marriage of money and brains for multiple and eugenic births seemed idyllic to everybody except two groups: the overstretched administration, which no longer knew whether the institution was on a spot of earth or diffused throughout the atmosphere; and the students, who knew thoroughly well that they were no longer the center of academic interest and concern. They could no longer acquire an education but must wrest it in fragments from an indifferent machine and assemble it for themselves. The observer from Mars would have summed up the state of affairs by saying that the values and practices of the free-for-all marketplace had conquered the academy.

This is where the story of Parsons College begins. It begins, paradoxically, with an impulse to go against the current, reinstate teaching, and prove that an institution devoted to the original idea of the College, a place concentrated upon one clear purpose, could succeed and earn a worthy reputation. It too would be providing "service"—service to the community —since the demand for bachelor's degrees was great and obvious: young people are a part of the community and they need educating. That particular service, one could argue, is not to be had as readily from a gas station or supermarket as from a college. The old college founders, including the churches, had a point.

But it is not easy in any modern society to do anything really different from what the great mass and its *geist* are bent upon. The reason is not that innovation is stopped by force or overt disapproval; the *corruptio* comes in with the promoters themselves; it seeps in through the cracks with the air that they breathe in common with the rest of the culture. Thus the regenerator of Parsons College, President Millard Roberts, brought with him (and by his actions unwittingly nurtured) all the bacteria that were afflicting all the colleges and universities of the postwar period: he was an advertiser, a public relations man, a skillful projector and magnifier of realities. He played up—how many of us can resist the temptation?—to the mental and moral weaknesses of the community, and the community responded: in a very short time Parsons was damagingly well-known.

His one lever and proof of virtue was money—he paid his faculty the highest salaries in the land; and his one idea of success was the quick and noisy boom—breaking the silence barrier. He applied with ferocity the oft-attempted notion of "using the plant" all the year round. He did what many other institutions talked of doing, which is to halt the proliferation of courses (late fruit of academic freedom) and stick to a stripped curriculum. He exacted hard work from his teachers and rewarded recruiters with bonuses, two things that many another place wished it had the nerve to do. He *acted* on the perfectly obvious perception that college buildings have become much too elaborate and plushy. He filled the lecture courses to overflowing, which was very bad of him, though it is all right when it happens at Berkvard or Wisconsota. He had the audacity to entrust section teaching to raw graduate students—bare B.A.'s. Did he not know that such exploitation and educational short-changing is a prerogative reserved for old-established places which are entitled to do it in the name of graduate scholarship?

In two respects he was ahead of the crowd: he went in for open admissions—come one, come all—thereby rescuing from academic extinction a good many students with poor records. And in this he showed a healthy distrust of scores and grades as they are produced by the current system. This second anticipation of recent ideas implied a flattering confidence in his staff. As President Patton said to a mother long ago: "Madam, we guarantee results—or we return the boy."

But the world was not prepared for this mixed flouting and flaunting of campus ways. The presiding genius spoke of his plan, but he had no plan. He spoke of profits from his operation, but there were no profits: he concealed his losses just like the big wealthy universities. He followed the ruling morality of survival and justification, which is not by faith or good works, but by turning intangibles into results,—any kind you want, on demand, quarterly, daily, oftener if you like; his results of course being as uncertain, not to say dubious, as in the big prosperous, prestigeful places. There the educational deficits are as well concealed as the financial, though they cannot be so much longer.

It would be unfair to Dr. Koerner's narrative to tell the reader how the plot comes out: it resembles a good thriller with a surprise ending which one has half-feared all along. But besides repeating my unfeigned praise of the masterly story-telling, I recommend to the reader that he watch at every turn for the tell-tale clues. As I hope to have shown, not everything that was done at Parsons was bad. But what was bad reflects the parlous condition of our higher education as a whole, and what was good reflects upon it. The sooner we see the state of affairs as a Great Depression in the world of values, the sooner reconstruction can begin.

Acknowledgments

This book depended on the willingness of hundreds of people to discuss a subject, Parsons College, that was uncomfortable for many of them. Some people did not want to be identified, and I have respected that desire. Some people understandably wished I would go away, but none declined entirely to talk. I am happy to say that all of the people I approached—present and past members of the Parsons faculty, the administration, the board of trustees, the student body, and a great many people outside Parsons—were at least cordial, most were quite cooperative, and many were eager to help. The book could hardly have been written without them, and to each of them I offer my sincere thanks.

To my research assistant, Susie Speakman Sutch, I am greatly indebted, not only for her patience in making lengthy and complex computations, but for her stamina in traveling with a tape recorder and other impedimenta to unlikely places in unlikely conveyances. Her help was indispensable and unfailingly cheerful. Several people read the book in manuscript: Alfred Ames, Dante Peter Ciochetto, Jack Mooney, Mortimer Smith, and George Weber. They made incisive criticisms and suggestions, most of which I acted on and for all of which I am extremely grateful. I absolve them, of course, from any responsibility for the book's shortcomings. And I am indeed grateful to Relm Foundation of Ann Arbor for its support of the project out of which this book came.

JDK

Contents

THE
Parsons College
BUBBLE

1: The Vaulting Ambition of Parsons College

> We are going to build the Harvard of the Midwest.
>
> —MILLARD ROBERTS

> We're a factory, that's all. But our product is a college education. A factory for educating kids.
>
> —MILLARD ROBERTS

> If Roberts had kept his mouth shut, he would have been regarded as a genius.
>
> —A PARSONS PROFESSOR

Late in the 1950's a bizarre chapter in the history of higher education in America began to unfold at an obscure college in the Midwest. It happened in the little town of Fairfield, Iowa, a sort of everyman's hometown. Fairfield lies in the southeastern part of the state in a stretch of rich rolling countryside that produces some of the world's best crops. Like many other country towns of the plains states, Fairfield evokes a nostalgic response from visitors. It has an assortment of small businesses, some light manufacturing, some grain elevators, a lot of retired farmers, and a neat square that would look like home to millions of Americans over thirty.

As the quiet, comfortable, conservative home of church-related Parsons College, Fairfield was an improbable backdrop for the playing out of a drama that took place there between 1955 and 1967 with a man named Millard George

Roberts on center stage throughout. The theme of the drama can be stated in the form of a few questions that colleges, no matter how desperate their plight, are rarely willing to ask themselves.

Can you run a college like a business? Can you give economic considerations first priority in making academic decisions? Can you apply the principles of cost accounting to the instructional program? Can you put the curriculum on a production line? Can you get college professors to agree that "productivity" is something they ought to worry about and that their personal productivity, meaning the number of students they teach, should be measured? Can you suppress the faculty's normal preoccupation with its rights and privileges to the point that the institution's president can direct the institution's affairs like the chief executive of a major corporation? Can you inject free enterprise, the profit motive in particular, into higher education? And if you do, can you make a profit?

The answer to these shocking and abrasive questions, if we are to judge by the experience of Parsons College, would seem to be "Yes," followed by a loud "But." The instinctive answer of educators, however, to such inquiries so crassly phrased would be a horrified "No!" Therefore the question of what the Parsons experiment proves or fails to prove is important, and I hope that the unenviable reputation developed by the college during the years of Roberts's administration will not permanently block a consideration of that experiment on its merits.

Up to 1955 Parsons College, like dozens of other small church-related institutions in the Midwest, had a history that was unexceptional and a reputation that was local. It had been established in the nineteenth century by a merchant of means who sought to bring God and opportunity together for the rural youth of an expanding nation. Louis B. Parsons of Utica, New York, died in 1855, assigning most of his estate, including 3,560 acres of "good Iowa land," to be used for the endowment of a college. For many years the Parsons College *Bulletin* (the college catalogue) began with this passage from the will of Louis Parsons:

> Having long been of the opinion that for the usefulness, prosperity and happiness of children, a good moral and intellectual or business education, with moderate means, was far better than large unlimited wealth . . . and having long been convinced that the future welfare of our country, the permanence of its institutions, the progress of our divine religion, and an enlightened Christianity, greatly depended upon the general diffusion of education under correct moral and religious influence, and having during my lifetime used, to some small extent, the means given me by my Creator in accordance with these convictions, and being desirous of still endowing objects so worthy as far as in my power lies, I do therefore . . . give and bequeath the residue of my estate . . . to my said executors and the survivors or survivor of them, in trust, to be used by them and expended in forwarding and endowing an institution of learning in the State of Iowa.

The execution of this characteristically American mandate was hampered by the Civil War and its aftermath. In 1874 the executors, having considered a number of sites in Iowa, accepted the invitation of Fairfield to locate the college there. Parsons College opened in 1875 as a sectarian but undogmatic institution affiliated with the Presbyterian Church. For more than three-quarters of a century thereafter, Parsons followed the course familiar to most small, impecunious colleges in America: it grew very slowly, taking any student who wanted to come; accumulating little endowment and many deficits; looking constantly to its trustees, the church, the local community, and scattered friends to keep it afloat; building an uncertain but loyal faculty on meager salaries; and from generation to generation offering the young people of its rural constituency an opportunity that had its limitations but was still an opportunity.

After years of up-and-down enrollments that reflected wars and depressions, Parsons arrived at the 1950's in a state of unusual debilitation. Enrollment was down to a few hundred, deficit financing was customary, salaries were ludicrously low, 80 per cent of the faculty held only a master's or bachelor's degree, and the physical plant was in a formidable state of disrepair. The condition of the college, that is, differed only in degree from that of many other small, church-related institutions. The college was not really on its last legs in the early 1950's, as is often alleged. Its relationship to the church was strong. Its debt was not large. It stood to profit from the nationwide upswing in college enrollments that was predicted. And there was a good *esprit de corps* within the faculty. The Parsons staff and faculty exhibited, as the head of the college noted in a letter in February, 1955, "an almost complete absence of that internal strife which is so often the bane of administrators," a condition that was to be reversed after 1955. But Parsons's situation, while far from hopeless, did require a fresh attack on old problems.

A Boomer Comes to Fairfield

The president of Parsons had resigned in 1954 and been replaced by an acting president for the 1954–1955 academic year while the board of trustees searched for a new president. A "Fifteen-Year Plan" for the growth and development of the college had been drawn up during this same year and had been formally adopted by the trustees in February, 1955,

a short time before they announced the results of their search
—the appointment of one Millard George Roberts as the new
president of Parsons College.

Who was Millard George Roberts? He was a Presbyterian
minister holding a junior position at the fashionable Brick
Presbyterian Church in New York City. Although he had had
no experience in educational administration, he did have
talents the Parsons trustees were after. They had decided
that what the college needed was a man with spirit and dash
who could do whatever was necessary to get more money
from donors and find more students. Other midwestern institutions had also stopped looking for scholars to fill their
presidential posts and had started looking for men with promotional abilities who could raise money and perhaps run the
schools efficiently.

The Parsons trustees had first approached an industrialist
friend of the college about the job, but he had declined. They
then turned their attention to Millard Roberts, who had been
suggested by Dean G. McKee, a Parsons alumnus who was also
a well-known minister and head of the Biblical Seminary in
New York City. McKee wrote to the trustees' search committee, characterizing Roberts as "a persuasive talker" and
saying:

> . . . Dr. Roberts's strong points are: 1) He comes near being
> a born promoter. He has ideas, and with them clear insight,
> as to ways and means for their realization. He understands
> publicity. . . . He has an excellent capacity for making
> contacts with people. . . . 2) He should have a grasp of
> what education is all about. . . . 3) As an ordained min-
> ister and a leader . . . in the church, he should be able to
> contribute much that is essential in making a church-
> related college what it ought to be. . . . He would quickly
> become a leader in church and academic circles in the Mid-
> west. . . . Not everyone will agree with him as his aggres-

siveness sometimes reaches too far too fast but, with a competent board of trustees to work with him, my judgment is that very substantial progress would be made if he were called to Parsons.

Other people also wrote to the search committee about Roberts, usually reinforcing McKee's appraisal. One of the Brick Church elders wrote, for example:

His duties have been in the administrative and financial areas, and he has performed them with outstanding success. . . . We have been impressed with his energy, his drive and his enthusiasm. . . . In discussing his future, some of us felt that his talents were in the field of administration, organization, fund raising and teaching, rather than in pastoral work. . . . I believe that he would bring to your college an enthusiasm, an administrative ability and experience in organization matters and fund raising that you would find valuable. . . .

The Parsons trustees also found Roberts "a persuasive talker." The chairman of the search committee, Walter Williams, publisher of the Fairfield paper, recalls that for his committee it was

tough to find a really good man who would accept. Roberts came out for a visit at our invitation and told us he thought he could get a million dollars within three months from one of his friends, Thomas Watson, Sr., chairman of IBM and an elder in the Brick Church. We were very impressed. When he became president of Parsons, Roberts actually got, I think, $250.00 from Watson.

Richard Hoerner, chairman of the board of trustees at the time, recalls that the gist of what people at the Brick Church seemed to be saying to the search committee was: "Roberts will be great if you can control him. If you can't, it will be a failure." At the meeting of the trustees that gave final approval to Roberts, one member apparently reflected the feelings of a number of trustees when he commented, "I don't think Dr. Roberts will last more than three or four years, but he is a salesman who can get us students and support."

With a certain open-eyed realism, then, the trustees of Parsons hired Millard Roberts, the plump Presbyterian minister from New York, to save the institution's body, not its soul. He was thirty-seven years old, a Republican and a Mason, a proven moneygetter and a promising manager, when he became the sixteenth president of the institution at the uninspiring salary of $8,700 a year, plus a house and an expense allowance of $1,200.

Roberts was born in a small village in upstate New York and had attended an unusual private secondary school, the Wyoming Seminary in Kingston, Pennsylvania, a co-educational boarding school. One of his teachers at the Seminary who was later brought to Parsons by Roberts, recalls Roberts the adolescent as "a short fat boy, full of ideas, very smart." After the Wyoming Seminary, Roberts had gone on to the University of Syracuse, and then had done work at Yale and the University of Chicago, which culminated in the Ph.D. degree in Divinity from Chicago in 1947. For his educational thesis he had written *The Methodist Book Concern in the West, 1800–1870*, an orthodox dissertation suitably ponderous and garlanded with elaborate footnotes and other scholarly apparatus. He had served in the army as a chaplain from 1943–1946 and had then done pastoral work at several churches before being appointed assistant to the minister of the Brick Presbyterian Church in 1952.

Roberts began his career at Parsons with a flamboyant inauguration put together with the help of a public relations firm at a cost that scandalized many friends of the ailing college and some of its trustees. A number of well-known educators and churchmen were flown to Fairfield for the ceremonies, including Eugene Carson Blake, General Secretary of the World Council of Churches, who gave the inaugural sermon and stressed the Christian mission of the college. Roberts's inauguration "was hailed," said the campus newspaper, "by persons and organizations in thirty-five states and seven foreign countries." It reported too that John Foster Dulles had sent regrets, explaining that his presence was required in Geneva. Roberts's "ascension," as it was quickly dubbed by the students, garnered some national publicity. It was an accurate augury of his administration.

For the next twelve years—until the bubble burst in 1967—"Bob" Roberts or "Dr. Bob," as he was often called, strove to build a national reputation for himself and the college. Which is a nice way of saying that he brought real enterprise and imagination to the art, if it is an art, of academic bally-hoo. Although most institutions of higher education pay attention to their own and their president's reputation, college promotional drives are usually conducted with some restraint; they rarely push an institution from obscurity to national prominence in a short time. But not so at Parsons. Roberts and the college were quickly thrust onto the national stage, though more as controversial than as heroic characters.

Roberts always had startling educational experiments to talk about in his travels, for grand ideas came and went at Parsons like the weather. He borrowed, adapted, or thought up a thousand educational notions that sounded exciting and promising when he talked about them. He tried them all at Parsons—ideas about how to run a college more efficiently than any had been run before; how to get students in quantity to come out to a college in the cornfields; how to lure the right kind of professors who would teach hard but would not rock the administration's boat; how to build cheap but serviceable buildings; how to make a college show a profit; how to start other colleges in Parsons's image; how to create corporations to receive consulting fees and to supply and service a nationwide commonwealth of colleges.

Roberts and the college were thus in a state of perpetual motion. Roberts's affinity for change was insatiable, his appetite for publicity boundless, and his capacity for alienating other educators remarkable. With the help of a private jet and public relations professionals, Roberts kept up an incredible pace. He not only ran the college, but also made innumerable local, regional, and national radio and television appearances. In addition he conducted a widespread consulting business, and he made enough speeches in any given year to fuel a presidential campaign.

Roberts's success on the promotional circuit was due to his ability to create events with high publicity potential and to extract the full publicity value from any given event. There was, for example, the occasion upon which the merchants and the chamber of commerce of Fairfield wanted to show their appreciation for the money that the new Parsons College was bringing into the community. Their appreciation took the form of a Cadillac for Roberts, though there seems to be a lingering question as to whether it was his own idea, that of a local plumber who did business with the college, or somebody else's.

Roberts's publicity campaign was also helped by the appealing personality he could turn on at will. He was a man of great persuasive talents. He had an ability to convince the unbelieving of quite improbable things, an ability to charm the uncommitted and disarm the hostile. However, there were always a few people on whom the charm did not work, men such as Walter Williams, the Fairfield trustee who headed the committee that had hired him, who comments: "I was off Roberts's team by February of his first year." Or William

DeMeester, president of one of the satellite colleges promoted by Roberts, who also claims to have seen through Roberts from the beginning. But the charm worked on most of the people Roberts met, certainly on the majority of newsmen, state legislators, parents, students, and visitors to the college.

When Roberts arrived at Parsons, the name of the college was hardly a household word in the United States, nor had it become one by the time he left a dozen years later. But both he and the college had acquired a considerable fame in the public arena and an even greater fame in the educational community. To many a businessman, philanthropist, and legislator, the name of Parsons College became a name to conjure with. To many a professor and college administrator, it became a name to spoil lunch with. There was also a large middle ground among the general public, where many laymen recognized the name of Parsons simply with curiosity. It was a name they associated with practices that sounded promising or novel or bizarre or vaguely questionable, but always interesting. There was not much middle ground, however, among educators—men who, it must be admitted, are rarely enthusiastic about changing their ways or about having them changed. To many educators, Parsons was a personal and professional threat. For them, a dispassionate consideration of the college was, and perhaps always will be, impossible.

In the end it was publicity that killed the college. It unleashed powerful groups in education against Roberts and Parsons. It even backfired in the popular press. Roberts used to say, when the publicity was not favorable, "Bad publicity is the best kind you can get." Bad publicity, however, precipitated the events that led to Judgment Day for Roberts and to the disaccreditation of Parsons by the regional accrediting agency, the North Central Association of Colleges and Secondary Schools, in the spring of 1967.

Parsons as the Lengthened Shadow of Its President

In contemplating the Parsons record, one inevitably thinks of Emerson's comment about an institution's being the length-ened shadow of one man. Certainly the history of Parsons from 1955 to 1967 is inextricably bound up with the public life of Millard Roberts. No amount of wishing can disentangle them so that they can be discussed separately, as many peo-ple would prefer. Roberts not only determined the policies of the college, but he also set the tone and temper, the style, the whole ethos of the institution. He needed a lot of help in carrying out his policies, and many other people share the responsibility for what happened at Parsons—the good and the bad. But as much as a college can ever be the mirror of a single man, Parsons was such an institution.

What, then, did the mirror show? Parsons was a place in continual ferment. I wish I could report that the ferment was educational and intellectual, but I am afraid it was more often a ferment of confusion and frustration. As one of Parsons's leading professors wrote to some of his colleagues in 1966, "To say that members of the Parsons College community work in a 'charged' atmosphere is probably the understate-ment of the year." The "charge" was emotional voltage much more often than it was educational current. Individual pro-fessors and departments sometimes did interesting things and achieved notable successes, but there was never the kind of inquiring spirit, campus zest, or intellectual excitement at Parsons that one might have expected at an institution that advertised itself so persistently as a center of innovation and experiment.

There was a high degree of insecurity at the college and a fast turnover of faculty. Although improvements were made toward the end, Roberts for most of his regime completely dominated the institution, exhibiting little tolerance for criticism or dissent. Raymond Gibson, provost of the college under Roberts in 1966–1967, wrote after leaving Parsons: "The faculty at Parsons had no freedom except to teach. Dissent with respect to curricula, administration, or policies established by the president was sufficient ground for censure; discrimination on pay, tenure, and promotions; and for termination at some convenient time."[1] Most important of all, perhaps, was the lack of institutional unity or dedication to a common purpose. Roberts was not a man to inspire unity and perhaps had no desire to do so. He frequently commented to his chief administrators, who themselves were subject to purges, that it was well to keep the faculty under pressure and fighting among themselves so that they would not then be fighting with the administration. One Parsons administrator said to me that "Roberts had a theory that the only way he could control the college was to keep everybody at everybody else's throat."

Also important in establishing the atmosphere at the college was Roberts's tendency to find subversion and conspiracy all around him. He was quickly suspicious, and so suspicion was always in the air at Parsons. "The place was full of stooges," says one Parsons professor, "always looking for something damaging against certain individuals." Roberts's suspicions reached a climax which almost seemed to justify his fears at one point in 1963–1964, when a kind of palace revolt discussed in Chapter 6 was staged by six faculty members with the behind-the-scenes assistance of a number of others. As a result, Roberts hired private detectives to investigate his faculty and staff. The investigators gave Roberts several hundred pages of reports which taken together draw a pretty full profile of what a lot of people thought about Parsons College. One man, a former FBI agent, was planted by Roberts within the college itself under the guise of a new employee brought in on a trial basis to help in fund raising. This "employee" eavesdropped, kept watch on certain individuals, rifled desks, brief cases, and wastebaskets, and checked certain homes at night. He solicited and recorded the opinions of dozens of members of the Parsons staff and faculty, local trustees, and townspeople about Parsons in general and the insurgent professors in particular—all under the pretense of his wanting only to get an honest picture of the college to help him decide whether to take the job permanently and move to Fairfield.

Another investigator, a woman from a Chicago detective agency, traveled around the country for a considerable time, interviewing prominent educators in addition to former Parsons professors (especially those who had revolted and quit, as well as their former neighbors and employers), and some Parsons trustees who might have been implicated in a plot against the college or might have known something about other trustees who were. She appeared before all of these obliging folk using a ruse that had at least the virtue of originality: she represented herself as having been hired by an anonymous philanthropist who was thinking of giving a substantial sum of money to Parsons. However, she would claim, he had heard some unfavorable rumors about the institution and wanted to get the considered opinions of a number of knowledgeable people as to whether this would be a wise gift. She successfully deceived almost all the people she talked to, while secretly taping some of the interviews and writing summaries of the rest.

Roberts was quick to admit to his chief administrators that his administrative theories owed something to Calvin, Machiavelli, and Nietzsche. This formidable trio of models may have been intended to neatly answer a lot of questions about his methods and is therefore probably suspect. It was supposed to explain Roberts's authoritarian style of administration; the antagonistic personal relations that he had with a number of individuals at Parsons (the charm he could exhibit with some people was matched by a legendary temper with others); and the generally frenetic, not to say tormented, way of life of the Parsons community. Certainly it would confuse judgment about the curious financial practices that were widely associated with the name of Parsons College.

And yet it cannot be denied that Roberts was a man who dreamed big and who went a considerable distance toward realizing his dreams. He had the virtue, as I suppose it to be, of never being intimidated by the novelty, the brazenness, or the scope of an idea. For a time he toyed, for example, with the idea of creating a complete educational system in Fairfield stretching from kindergarten through the Ph.D. Then he thought of creating an extensive system of satellite colleges modeled on Parsons and dependent on Parsons for various kinds of services, for which they would pay. He succeeded in inspiring no fewer than six communities in the Midwest to found such colleges, and he had plans for more.

Together with seven other people, including such figures as Earl J. McGrath (former United States Commissioner of Education) and Theodore A. Distler (former president of the Association of American Colleges), he operated an organization called Consultants, Inc., to which the satellite colleges and a number of other institutions paid consulting fees. Consultants, Inc., however, was dissolved within two years of its inception because several participants were dissatisfied with the uses to which the corporation was being put.

Roberts dreamed of a corporation that dozens, perhaps hundreds, of colleges would be persuaded to look to for centralized services of many kinds—the training of recruiters and other types of personnel, the computerized search for students and faculty members, the buying of everything from meat to janitorial supplies. Under the right circumstances, there might be persuasive economic arguments in favor of such an organization, and Roberts quietly established the Foundation for American Education (incorporated in 1966 in Illinois). It was, Roberts now admits, "a front" for finding students for Parsons and the sister colleges. However, it too was dissolved before it was well begun because of the unenthusiastic response of colleges and administrators Roberts had hoped would be his clients.

Roberts dreamed of running a vast educational empire from his estate in Oneonta, New York, where, as chancellor of a great private university system, he would preside over a graduate school that would be fed by a commonwealth of affiliated colleges. As one of his former colleagues, now at one of the satellite colleges, comments:

> Roberts would go on and on painting this utopian picture of colleges throughout the country that were going to be opened under his guidance in Ohio, Florida, everywhere. There was going to be a hotel in New York where his professors with $50,000 salaries would live. He went on and on. It was *so* far out.

These dreams of wealth and grandeur evolved and changed rapidly. They were not always limited to education. Roberts was stung from time to time by political ambition. At one point he seriously considered running for the governorship of Iowa, but realized that nomination by either party would be, to say the least, improbable. A position in national politics was even more improbable, though Milford Hughes, one of Roberts's closest subordinates at Parsons, comments that "Roberts would have gone to Washington as almost anything." It is interesting, if a bit unsettling, to speculate how far Roberts's special talents would have taken him if he had made it to Washington. But mainly Roberts's dreams seemed to center on ways in which he could exploit his work at Parsons in order to build new worlds in education. And he might really have built some had he moved with less speed and with much less noise. Why he did not do so remains unanswered, even by Roberts himself. In 1967, after he had been fired from Parsons, I asked Roberts why he had not worked in a more politic fashion at Parsons, and he replied, "I don't know. I can't pronounce on my motives." In 1969, at the end of another long interview, Roberts admitted to me that he had made a lot of mistakes at Parsons, especially tactical and political mistakes, and that he had not always stuck to the facts in his speeches and promotional operations. He attributed his mistakes to his relative youth and inexperience and added that he would now do many things differently. "But we all," he said, "have 20–20 vision hindsight."

Perhaps the word *ambition* best characterizes the Parsons story. Ambition of course can be a constructive force in education, one that gets things done, although it may not be cordially received by a profession which is inherently conservative and devoted to the status quo. Ambition can also be a consuming and destructive force. It can be, in Macbeth's line, "vaulting ambition, which o'erleaps itself." Too often it was vaulting ambition that prevailed at Parsons. But ultimately the reasons for Parsons's institutional behavior under Roberts may be too illusive and complex for clear, precise analysis. No doubt Coleridge was right in saying that "No man ever does anything from a single motive"—much less a collection of people constituted as a college.

Most people would agree that both Roberts and Parsons College under his administration were a unique phenomenon. American education was not "ready" for them. For many educators, what was unique about Parsons was what was bad about it. One well-known university administrator was probably reflecting a consensus of American educators' views when he wrote to me: "What was good at Parsons was not new and what was new was not good." While I can easily appreciate that view, I don't share it. The problem is to separate the good from the bad, to separate the valuable experiments from the frailties of the individuals who attempted them, and that is the aim of the rest of this book.

NOTE

[1] Raymond Gibson, "The Scholarch of Parsons and the NCA," *Phi Delta Kappan* (June, 1968), p. 589.

2: The Theory and Practice of Profit at Parsons

Not the least charm of a theory is that it is refutable.

—NIETZSCHE

Half the truth is often a great lie.

—POOR RICHARD

I do not mind lying, but I hate inaccuracy.

—SAMUEL BUTLER

"Profit," said Millard Roberts in a speech in 1962, "is a dangerous word in college management." He never made a truer statement or one that he forgot more often. Or perhaps he did not really forget it; perhaps, as one Parsons professor suggested, Roberts flung the word "profit" around almost deliberately, needling his peers among college presidents. Certainly one of Roberts's most offensive habits in the eyes of other educators was his constant use of the word *profit* in public. He got a great deal of local and national press coverage on this point, the fruit of an enormous amount of time he invested in traveling and speech-making. He was always turning up somewhere telling businessmen, rotary clubs, chambers of commerce, legislators, and academic gatherings how profitable Parsons College was and how profitable other colleges could be if they followed his example—and that they had better follow his example if they wanted to survive.

Now, the whole idea of a college's making a profit is unsavory to many, perhaps most, educators. It isn't done. It violates one of their strongest convictions. A nonprofit institution that brags about making money seems to them a contradiction in terms and might even call the tax-exempt status of the institution into question. When Roberts talked about his college "making millions," educators were not merely profoundly irritated; they strongly suspected that it could not be true. People who knew educational finance knew that Parsons could not be doing what it seemed to be claiming.

There were times, however, when Roberts recanted and promised one group of people or another, such as visiting accreditation teams and meetings of college presidents, that he would stop talking about profit. But he found the promise difficult to keep. The word remained part of the Roberts rhetoric to the end. John O. Hall, director of institutional research at the University of Pittsburgh and himself author of an early study of Parsons, recalls that "the day before Roberts was fired, he gave a speech at the Pittsburgh Rotary Club in which he stated how much profit he was making. I was at that luncheon. After all these years, he still was insisting on using the word 'profit.' " Whether it was a calculated provocation or not, Roberts, as an itinerant speechifier and evangelist for what he called the Parsons Plan, often failed to tell all the relevant facts about the finances of the college.

The Parsons Plan is itself something of a misnomer, although people use it as a convenient bit of shorthand. There was never actually a "plan" in the sense that a coherent, carefully developed system of college management was created at Parsons. What was created was a series of rather haphazard trial-and-error experiments, some of which succeeded, more or less, and which eventually added up to something people called a plan. There are elements of these experiments that might be applicable separately to many American institutions, and all of them taken together might be turned into some kind of logical package for adoption by some private colleges that are in financial trouble. It was not so much a plan as a group of complementary and expedient procedures and controls, but I too will call it a plan for the sake of convenience.

The main goal of the Parsons Plan was, of course, the survival of a private college in an educational economy increasingly dominated by tax-supported institutions, an economy in which the traditional sources of gifts were not adequate to meet rising costs. Private institutions could get off the backs of donors and out of the slough of poverty and could pay their way by relying primarily on student fees while at the same time successfully competing with public institutions.

"Current income" colleges are nothing new in the United States. Many private institutions meet their operating expenses chiefly out of student fees and have done so for many years. But Roberts saw, no doubt rightly, that the future for such colleges was going to be tougher than the past and that they were not going to compete and survive unless they made some major changes in the way they did business. Roberts made this pitch in a variety of ways, usually in a canonical tone. In his speeches he would offer, for example, a quick history of the development of institutions of higher education and how the independent institutions got themselves into their present dilemma:

> The combination of accrediting association which had no long-term goals of measurement, and small colleges which had no goals excepting survival, left a sorry pattern among colleges which were among the oldest in their sections of the country. . . . Meanwhile, the great state institutions of the country had become "prestige" colleges of the first order. . . . The students in the state universities found everything better, and it cost them less. The independent colleges were in an impossible business position, for their competitors were selling a better product, in both academic excel-

lence and in social prestige, and *they were selling it for less than half the price.*[1]

Or he would adopt an apocalyptic stance, like this:

> Either the small independent colleges will double and triple their budgets for professors' salaries in the next few years, or they will die. When the tax-supported colleges and universities are joined by hundreds of junior colleges and community colleges now being born, the bidding for professors will reach a fever pitch. Small independent colleges will find their good men leaving, and they will be left with the dregs of the profession.[2]

Or he would offer a statistical analysis of birth rates and enrollments to prove the need for rapid expansion of private colleges, provided they could free themselves of deficit budgets and dependence on dwindling endowment income:

> . . . the enrollment bulge brings every independent college to its "moment of truth." If it expands its enrollment, it doubles its deficit. If it raises its charges, it prices itself out of the market. If it stands pat, it loses its faculty. . . . Independent colleges have only one advantage in this ponderous pattern, and unless they use it they will die by the hundreds within the next thirty years.[3]

The "advantage" he had in mind was, of course, more efficient operation along the lines of the Parsons Plan. Roberts talked a lot about injecting corporate business practices into education to achieve this increased efficiency. He would say, for instance:

> Business men know they will succeed if they can produce a better product for less money. This is the core test every

corporation faces every day. Perhaps we had better begin to use corporate practices in the field of education, to get better quality for less money.[4]

He also talked a lot about "cost accounting" as the key to Parsons's success, though most of the other Parsons administrators did not seem very sure of what he meant. In 1966 Roberts welcomed a blue-ribbon delegation of visitors to Parsons from Wisconsin, which included the governor, state legislators, and educators, with the statement, "Cost accounting is the basis of everything you'll see here." But when the delegation talked to the Parsons business manager, they were told, "I don't know what he's talking about."

The problem as usual was semantic. Roberts really did have a talent for certain kinds of fiscal analysis and projection and did institute some controls at Parsons that could legitimately be called cost accounting; but in important areas of management he was, by universal agreement, magnificently inefficient. Robert W. Williams, vice president for business affairs at Parsons, puts the matter this way:

> Cost control as Roberts talked about it is deceiving because on many things such as simple systems control, he was grossly lax. But in terms of having concepts and working them out, in having to figure out the unit cost, the student-faculty ratio, the number of courses the school could afford to offer, the economic effect of controlling curriculum, how this would affect revenues that would then be available for something else—Roberts did more work of this kind than any other college president I know of. He worked at it constantly.

The main elements of the Parsons Plan as Roberts and his consultants developed them over the years were:

1. Year-round operation
2. An open-door admissions policy with intensive recruit-ment
3. Sharply restricted curriculum with large classes
4. High teaching loads and high salaries
5. High tuition and fees
6. Cheap buildings with the fullest possible use of them

Most of these measures had been recommended to Roberts and the Parsons trustees by Ralph Cooper Hutchison in an ex-haustive financial study of the college in 1959. In three reports to the college, Hutchison presented a plan that, as he put it,

> points out for Parsons College what might be achieved through the courageous utilization of its own teaching re-sources; how Parsons might, within present resources, dou-ble and in some cases triple faculty salaries; may develop and employ outstanding professors in fewer subjects, ad-vance academic standards, improve scholarly training and yet develop an annual operating surplus instead of a deficit. . . . That Parsons can achieve this and at the same time become a much greater college academically is the convic-tion of this study.[5]

Although many of Hutchison's recommendations may have sounded utopian to the Parsons trustees in 1960, they were put into effect and ultimately became a large part of the Par-sons Plan.

Curiously enough, one of Hutchison's recommendations that was not accepted was that the college make use of instruc-tional television; and the reader will look in vain in this book for any discussion of the use of educational technology at Parsons. There wasn't any. One would suppose that Parsons, by putting such emphasis on educational efficiency, would have made great use of closed-circuit television or teaching machines or that it would have experimented with computer-assisted instruction, films, and other applications of electronics and technology to education. Parsons shunned this entire field for reasons that are not clear. Parsons professors did, however, make very extensive use of multiple-choice tests that could be run through and graded on the college's data processing equipment.

Suppose we look at each of the elements listed above and at what it contributed to the plan.

Year-Round Operation

Although Parsons was one of the first colleges in the country to make a serious attempt at year-round operation and continues to do so today, the idea was hardly new when the college took this step in 1960. There had been discussion off and on for many years in the United States about the possible efficiencies of year-round operation of educational establishments. But few institutions at any level of the educational system, except "proprietary" institutions such as technical and business schools that need to show a profit, have ever adopted a twelve-month or even an eleven-month calendar.

The late 1950's and early 1960's was one of the "on" periods of discussion of this proposal. A number of colleges seemed ready to convert to year-round operation. The idea was given a strong push by Beardsley Ruml in 1959 in his *Memo to a College Trustee*. The next year the case for year-round operation was made with considerable force by Grayson Kirk, then president of Columbia University. His case seems to me at least as valid today—although Kirk, in view of his adventures with student rebels at Columbia in 1968, might well have second thoughts about having a full complement of students on campus all summer. In 1960 he said:

> It is a wry commentary on our colleges, presumably the incubators of progressive ideas, that they are operating on a schedule geared to the seventeenth century. Four years still is the prescribed period for earning a bachelor's degree in the arts and sciences, despite decisive evidence that such a leisurely pace falls far short of utilizing efficiently the students' capacity and the schools' facilities. Four years in some adolescent playpens that are called centers of learning may be a pleasant interlude for young people, but it is a luxury which they, their parents, the colleges and the country no longer can afford.
>
> . . . there is a logical remedy for this costly time lag. It is the trimester plan for completing college in three years by dividing the school calendar into three terms of fifteen weeks each instead of the two sixteen-week semesters which now occupy energetic youngsters only 180 days a year. . . . The three-year college is not a new proposal. It flourished a half century ago at Harvard.
>
> . . . In compiling the material for this article, I wrote to Dr. [James Bryant] Conant, asking whether his opinion [on the three-year college] has changed. His reply, dated December 10, 1959, follows in part:
>
> "I am as enthusiastic about the three-year program as I was nearly fifty years ago when, as an undergraduate, I took advantage of it at Harvard [which had a three-year degree at that time]. . . . You may wonder why I did not do something to forward this idea when I was president of Harvard for twenty years. In a word, the Harvard atmosphere had been so completely changed by Mr. Lowell [A. Lawrence Lowell, Conant's predecessor] that a four-year curriculum was one of those sacred cows which I inherited and could not be touched, let alone moved."[6]

The first institution to put a trimester system into operation was the University of Pittsburgh, which converted to it in September, 1959, nine months ahead of Parsons. It did so for the same reason as Parsons: to be able to take in more students and more fees without a proportional expansion in buildings and facilities. In a word, to operate more efficiently. The trimester system has not been a resounding success at Pittsburgh. It has been well supported by graduate students, many of whom do not or cannot share the undergraduates' devotion to a long summer vacation and who are wont to attend summer school in any case. But the summer trimester has not attracted undergraduates in sufficient numbers to make it a financially sound operation. Pittsburgh nevertheless continues with the system (having split the summer trimester into two segments for greater appeal to students) and still hopes to make it pay its way.

Parsons had one enormous advantage over Pittsburgh. It was in a position to compel some of its students, who perhaps were afraid that they could not be admitted to other colleges, to attend the summer trimester. It could thereby insure better enrollment than could Pittsburgh, where students were not forced into the summer term. Parsons required new applicants with low grade point averages to come in the summer if they wanted to be admitted in the fall. It also required students who had done badly in the fall or spring trimesters and whose grade point averages were sufficiently low to attend the following summer to make repairs in their records. That was the policy, but there were always differences between policy and practice at Parsons. The college might have threatened students with dismissal or nonadmittance if they did not attend the summer trimester, but it was apt to let them in anyhow for the regular fall term—a fact that did not escape many students who were being pressured to sign up for the summer.

Many educators would regard with distaste the practice

of requiring students to attend a summer term. Some would think of it as a callous policy, some perhaps as unethical. Some would speak of the Parsons policy as one of black-jacking students for money. I don't share that view. It seems to me entirely reasonable for a college to say to its marginal students that it will admit them only if they help keep the institution solvent by attending one or another trimester as stipulated by the college. The student is free to accept this condition or not, just as he is free to accept or not all of the other conditions that colleges lay down for students.

If one considers this to be discrimination against weaker students, so presumably would be all of the other require-ments made by colleges that students have to meet to remain in good standing and to graduate. I see little difference be-tween the Parsons policy and that of some unquestioned in-stitutions that have "delayed enrollment" plans whereby marginal students are made to wait until the February semester if they want to attend the institution at all. One should also remember that the practice of requiring students with deficient records to attend college the summer before their regular fall enrollment is not at all uncommon in American institutions.

However, coercing students into a summer session might have bad effects on the quality of work they do. If they are so resentful of the policy that they refuse to maintain a decent level of performance, or if they adopt a belligerent okay-I'm-here-now-teach-me attitude, the college has a problem. Parsons had this problem and never found a solution to it.

In addition, as is so often the case when one tries to defend some of the policies and practices at Parsons, one must make room for possible abuses. If, for example, a Parsons admis-sions counselor used fear to induce students to attend the summer trimester—perhaps by telling his parents that the college had hundreds or thousands more applicants than it could possibly admit in the fall and that their son had better get in early by attending the summer trimester or face the possibility of not getting in at all—then there is clearly no defense for the college. Or if the college required students to continue to attend summer after summer when the institution knew that it could do little or nothing for them, there is likewise no defense.

If the college's promotional literature misled readers into thinking that more personal counseling and tutoring were available than was true, or led them to think that a well-developed junior-year-abroad program or a work-study program was available—all of which is strongly suggested in the flyers sent out by Parsons when it announced its conversion to a trimester calendar in June, 1960—no defense is possible. But such abuses do not seem to me to negate the general view that an institution ought to have the right to require certain students under certain circumstances to attend summer school.

Both the hard and the soft sell, however (including a reduced tuition plan based on grades), were never enough at Parsons to make the summer trimester the equal of the other two trimesters. It always had the lowest enrollment and failed most of the time to pay its full way. Because there was always a high concentration of poor students in the summer, the level of work did not match that of the other trimesters. Parsons suffered, that is, from the same problems that other institutions on the trimester plan suffer from, but somewhat less so in regard to the most important of these problems, enrollment.

In spite of the problems, it seems to me that Parsons did establish the economic and educational validity of year-round operation, whether on a trimester or some other calendar. Parsons's experience lends strong support to the theoretical arguments: year-round operation does allow the ambitious student to complete his degree in two and two-thirds years (eight trimesters) and to be out earning money (and paying taxes) well over a year before students in conventional programs. If the three trimesters are organized appropriately, they allow the student three different points of entry into college (a time-saving convenience for veterans, transfer students, and special students) and can be so arranged as to coincide with high school graduations. All core or lower division courses can be offered every trimester, thus allowing students to do their work on whatever kind of yearly schedule fits their personal circumstances, including outside jobs. But the main advantage demonstrated at Parsons is allowing the institution to operate more efficiently than it could on a semester basis.

Why then don't more institutions move to a year-round operation? I don't know. Currently only about 3 per cent of American colleges operate on a trimester or some other year-round calendar. One would suppose that tax-supported institutions in particular would do so. One would suppose that state legislatures would compel public colleges and universities—not to mention public schools—to adopt a plan of full operation the year around in view of the financial advantages, to say nothing of the unsatisfied demands for education in most states. Perhaps legislatures have been taken in by the propaganda, or dissuaded by the recalcitrance of educators themselves. Perhaps some legislatures do not feel strongly enough about the economies to be realized through year-round operation to fight this particular battle. The nine-month academic year is practically unassailable, and educators themselves, who ought to be strong supporters of greater efficiency, especially if it means higher salaries, have constructed many spurious but seemingly plausible arguments as to why institutions can't really operate on a year-round schedule or can't save much money if they do.

In brief, Parsons did demonstrate that the trimester system has important financial and educational advantages, provided only that students can be required or persuaded to attend in the summer. But I don't know whether that fact will interest very many people in higher education.

Open Admissions with Intensive Recruitment

In a later chapter I will detail the high priority Roberts gave to increasing Parsons's enrollment and the lengths to which the school went to achieve this increase. Roberts knew that *volume* was important to the economics of the plan, for it is only when an institution has reached a "critical mass" (as the physicists say) in the size of its student body that profit margins begin to mean anything. A college of a few hundred students could not succeed with the Parsons Plan. Unfortunately, however, Parsons was too successful in recruiting students and went far beyond the critical mass. As more students arrived, more buildings and facilities had to be created, more faculty members hired, more of everything provided, and therefore more loans had to be negotiated to pay for it all.

In spite of the desire of many people at Parsons, including many trustees, to slow down or to stop the rate of growth and to have a period of consolidation, Roberts would not agree to easing the pace. He kept pushing for more students. He liked to demonstrate mathematically that the college could not stop, that it would go broke if his increasing enrollment projections were not met. Parsons therefore found itself on a high-speed treadmill that needlessly compromised the pay-as-you-go principle which Roberts was trying to establish—but more of that later. Suffice it at this point to say that a sizeable but not constantly increasing student body—one of perhaps two or three thousand—is essential to the economics of the Parsons Plan.

Sharply Restricted Curriculum with Large Classes

I will discuss this subject at length in Chapter 3 and so I will not linger over it here except to emphasize that both elements (few courses and large classes) are important. There must be, that is, an inviolable nonproliferation treaty between the administration and the faculty that puts well-recognized limits around the number of courses that will be permitted. There must also be agreement that large lecture classes are to prevail, especially in the years of greatest student enrollment, the first two years.

High Teaching Loads and High Salaries

Perhaps the point of greatest notoriety about Parsons, certainly within professorial circles, was the salary scale. The college became famous when it started turning up near the top of national salary tabulations alongside such institutions as Harvard and the University of Chicago. One such tabulation is published each year by the American Association of University Professors. For a while Parsons, in supplying information to the AAUP, counted only the salaries of its "ranked faculty," not those of its "preceptors" or "tutors," thus keeping the average salary high—although it reversed itself in calculating its student-teacher ratio and had a tendency to count everybody on the staff, thus keeping that figure low. The AAUP eventually required the college to lump together the ranked faculty and preceptors, but even when Parsons complied, its position remained at or near the national top for salaries during the latter years of Roberts's administration.

Specifically, the average faculty salary when Roberts arrived at Parsons was about $3,600. When he departed it was about $12,000 if one counts all teaching members of the three classes of staff. Counting only the "ranked faculty," the average was around $18,000, with a range that stretched from $10,000, to $35,000, not including fringe benefits. The average for "preceptors" was a little over $10,000 and the range was from $7,000 to $15,000. The average for "tutors" was a little over $6,000 and the range from $5,000 to $8,000. Thus the salaries of Parsons's teachers in 1966–1967 for teaching two-thirds of a year reached from $5,000 to $35,-000. If one includes fringe benefits the top professor's salary would be about $40,000.

Roberts felt that high salaries would relieve the staff of any necessity to moonlight and would allow them to give their full attention to what he wanted them to do: teach. A candid assessment of the Parsons staff, however, would suggest that many of its members, even granted the special circumstances of teaching at Parsons, were overpaid. The college paid many of them more than was necessary to get and keep them, and far more than they could have commanded anywhere else. Why the institution was needlessly extravagant is an interesting question. Perhaps Roberts valued the publicity of having Parsons seem to compete with Harvard and Chicago. Also, the college's contract with Roberts called for him to receive twice the salary of the school's highest paid professor.

At any rate, his policy on salaries was not an unmixed blessing. Although high salaries are an important part of the Parsons Plan, they could be considered to "work" only if they attracted exceptionally good people. If they attracted people interested solely in the salary, the policy would have to be called a failure. The issue of course is not that clear-cut, for Parsons attracted a variety of people. That the salaries did bring in a number of dubious people is a matter of common agreement. William DeMeester, who was one of the most respected and outspoken department heads at Parsons, is reflecting no more than customary sentiment in this comment:

> I would say that 1961 and 1962 was the start of the big surge in salaries. Roberts then started to hire people at salaries so far above what they were used to, and would then brag publicly about it, that many of the people already on campus who were doing a really dedicated job felt they were being overlooked. I heard ———— [a Parsons administrator] make the comment one day on the telephone: "Well, we've got enough work horses right now—what we need are some show horses." I was in his office one day when he was talking on the phone with someone in the East explaining that he was looking for a $25,000 or $30,000 a year man. Roberts had the idea that if you paid a man twice as much as he was making, he would be twice as good. Most of the people that went to Parsons under those conditions went there quite simply because the salary was better than at any place else open to them, and that was a poor reason. They were attracted by that monthly paycheck rather than by the basic philosophy of working with average kids. . . .

Another Parsons-watcher—one who is not an educator but has an intimate knowledge of the institution—makes this astringent comment:

> I think that many of the faculty members were just interested in the dollars. You can see it in the number that left when the college got into financial difficulty. After watching Parsons, I no longer put much faith in the com-

ments I hear about the altruism of academicians, and how willing they are to give of themselves for the good of the country or their students . . . in the main they are just as greedy as the greediest businessman, only they work less.

Not a few present and former Parsons professors are frank to admit that the Parsons salaries were the main factor in their decision to join the college, though most also cite the Parsons program as having influenced them. Here is a fairly typical comment from a former professor and administrator: "The contract that Roberts offered me was so high that I felt in the interest of my family I should take it. I was also intrigued by the philosophy that he had there. So I decided to make the greatest mistake of my life and go to Parsons."

Parsons's administrators were probably the most highly paid in the country. An academic vice president at $50,000 and other administrators at $45,000 and $40,000 were beyond their counterparts at even the richest colleges and universities. Roberts himself started at Parsons at a very modest $8,700 a year plus a few fringes. By the time he was fired, he had reached an annual salary, including fringe benefits and tax-sheltered items, of about $75,000. With his consulting fees and innumerable speaking engagements that grew out of his work at Parsons, his income, at well over $100,000 a year, possibly outdistanced the earned income of any other college or university president in the country.

Roberts was a believer in personal incentives—obviously. Not only did he pay many of his faculty and staff members more than was necessary, but he also used other gimmicks to keep up their "productivity." He added escalator clauses, for example, to their contracts, stating that they were to receive stipulated increases each year over a period of years —a highly unusual arrangement in the academic world. He also made a sort of productivity analysis of both departments and individual professors with a view to adjusting expenditures and contracts on the basis of the results. He would tabulate, that is, the number of students and credit hours "produced" by each department and put that against the costs involved, mostly salaries, and would then rank order the departments according to their productivity and also according to the number of "D's" and "F's" given by the departments.

On this sort of calculation, the most productive departments were often History, Philosophy-Religion, Art, and Humanities, and the least productive English and the sciences. A high rank in the productivity index often but not always matched up with a high rank in the tabulation of grades (high meaning a low number of "D's" and "F's" and therefore more productive). The Education department, for example, might rank highest in the grade tabulation, having given the fewest "D's" and "F's," but relatively low in overall productivity.

When Roberts applied this system not only to departments but to individuals, calculating how much "tuition income" (that is, the number of students taught) was produced by each professor or staff member, he was once again in very unpopular territory. The college ran studies on how many students appeared before each professor and how much tuition income each professor was therefore producing for the college. The economics of the plan called for a professor to produce three times his salary in tuition income. Although Roberts was strongly criticized for this practice, I again do not share what is probably the majority view in higher education. I see nothing wrong with a college that is trying to pay its way out of tuition and fees keeping a close watch on the contribution that its professors and departments make to that end. Indeed if more colleges worried about such matters, they might have fewer deficits and quite possibly better programs. What a college administration does with such information is another thing, but I can see nothing wrong with its gathering the data. Yet the idea of a professor's having to "pay his way" within his own institution, or even of his being apprised of how far short of it he falls, somehow strikes many if not most educators as quite improper.

In exchange for a high salary, Roberts expected high productivity, no research, no moonlighting (which was not much of an option anyhow in Fairfield, Iowa), and dedication to teaching. Most contracts called for two trimesters of teaching a year, allowing one full trimester off out of three for research and travel. Roberts did not break any traditions in the matter of teaching loads. If anything, the trimester off was unusually generous as well as exceedingly expensive. He did try from time to time to induce people to teach a third trimester without additional pay and some did so year after year, but in general the two-thirds arrangement prevailed. Nor was the teaching load during the trimesters that one was on campus as onerous as is widely believed. The average was twelve to fifteen hours, meaning four or five classes that met three times a week. This is high by current standards at the best institutions and had to be to make the system work. But it was not excessive, nor is it higher than what is still required today by many institutions far down the salary scale. If anything made the Parsons teaching load heavy, it was the fact that so many courses were primarily formal lectures to large groups of students, as well as the fact that Roberts required the faculty to maintain office hours for purposes of student consultation for most of the day—a practice extremely rare in higher education and one that would horrify most professors. So, in general, the Parsons professor worked hard for his high salary, but he was hardly enslaved.

High Tuition and Fees

Parsons could afford to charge higher fees than most other second-rank colleges because it had a clientele that was to some extent captive. Many of its students felt, although they were wrong, that given their academic records, Parsons was the only school that would admit them. Other students simply did not want to look any further. Still others were recruited in the East from affluent families and were not much worried about the fees. Parsons accurately assessed its market and pegged its fees accordingly. It did not charge all the market would bear and was not exorbitant in its fees, but Parsons was on the high side of the national scale and higher than other colleges with which it might be thought to compete. Table 2–1 shows tuition and fees during Roberts's administration (there were various special fees in addition to these).

As can be seen, the college at the time of Roberts's departure was charging an inclusive fee of about $2,300 for a

TABLE 2–1

Trimester Fees at Parsons College, 1955–1967

	TUITION	ROOM	BOARD	GENERAL FEE
1955–1956	$185	$ 90	$190	$40
1956–1957	200	100	200	40
1957–1958	225	100	200	40
1958–1959	225	125	225	50
1959–1960	275	125	225	50
1960–1961	300	150	250	50
1961–1962	350	175	260	50
1962–1963	400	200	275	50
1963–1964	450	200	300	50
1964–1965	550	200	300	60
1965–1966	550	200	300	60
1966–1967	600	200	300	60

normal academic year and $3,400 for a full year of three trimesters. But the college did not collect the full amount from every student, for there were scholarships and special circumstances that reduced the charges for some students, and bills were uncollectable from some others. These fees, while not as low as those of small, church-related colleges (to which people are prone to compare Parsons), were high but not excessive. And Parsons was not a small, church-related college in the latter years of Roberts's administration.

Thanks to the tuition and fees at Parsons, a substantial amount of "excess income" was created and was augmented by a variety of related operations encompassing everything from the college bookstore (a prime source of "profit" on many campuses) to the snack bar and pinball machines. In most of the leading private colleges, tuition and fees for board and room produce somewhere between 40 and 50 per cent of general income. At Parsons they produced 95 per cent, which was probably more than they produce even at other current income institutions. At tax-supported institutions, they produce only 10 to 15 per cent of general income. It might come as a shock to many parents and students to know that their favorite college makes money on board and room as well as on books and other enterprises, but these sources of income are more important today than ever before in private institutions. Parsons simply demonstrated that even more money could be made from them.

Cheap Buildings

More than any other single factor, the problem of buildings gave Roberts and the Parsons Plan the greatest trouble. It is one thing to run a college out of tuition and fees—to pay, that is, current operating expenses out of operating income—but a far different thing to *finance* a college out of this income; to buy equipment and put up buildings as well as to meet the daily operating costs. But Roberts was out to prove that total financing out of fees was possible. That was his whole pitch: the need for colleges to move away from dependence on endowment and gifts and to rely solely on income from students. Most educators did not then and do not now believe that colleges can be so financed.

At Parsons the constant increase in enrollment kept the college in a financial bind. Roberts's refusal to get off the treadmill meant that he was faced every year with the necessity of providing more housing, more classroom space, and more of everything else for the additional students who were expected to enroll the next year. But one thing he could not do was to extract enough money out of current income in any one year to meet the staggering costs of new buildings needed for the next year. What he could do, if he could find the necessary lenders, was to borrow the money needed for buildings and try to meet the long-term interest payments out of current funds. He was convinced that Parsons and other colleges could amortize all the buildings they needed out of income if they would mend some of their managerial ways.

One of their ways that needed mending was their devotion to elaborate and expensive buildings—"monuments," as Roberts called them, "to the vanity of adults." Education did not need to be conducted, he would say, in an environment of "pillars and pomp"; the purpose of a college education "is not greatly aided by high spires, vaulted ceilings, and marble exteriors." He upheld his spartan convictions by putting up a collection of buildings at Parsons whose plainness would be hard to match on other campuses. He liked to brag that he constructed buildings for twelve dollars a square foot, which is half or a third of the costs at other institutions, and that he completely carpeted and air-conditioned them to boot. But he did not add that cheap construction means high maintenance and that he calculated his square-foot costs in unorthodox ways. Nor did he point out that you reach diminishing financial returns when students accidentally start putting their feet through the walls. A visitor to Parsons might submit that the human soul requires an occasional window or two (some of Roberts's buildings had none), and might observe that elbow room was at a minimum in Roberts's buildings, and that the total result of his approach to buildings was as unlovely a bit of construction as anybody would care to contemplate. Nor did Roberts add that serious overcrowding was a chronic condition in the Parsons dormitories. On one occasion it was even necessary temporarily to put up students on cots in an old gymnasium. For years some of the students had to live two to a room that had been designed for one and three to a room that had been designed for two— a condition not unknown on other fast-growing campuses but not as persistent as it was at Parsons.

Roberts was never out of trouble with his buildings. He did have astonishing success in negotiating large loans from prime lenders, though no substantial loans were made by local banks. It must have required a major act of faith on the part of the lenders, but Roberts could be a persuasive man. He could "prove" with pencil and paper the economies of his plan and his ability to pay back big loans on schedule, all based on projections of a growing student body, growing income, and a large "cash flow." It was presumably these happy projections that the Parsons lenders were buying when they put up large loans. Even these loans were not enough, however, to meet the building requirements; so that Roberts had to move funds regularly from the general account into "plant."

In short, Roberts produced no miracles in buildings. He did put up buildings more cheaply than other colleges but they were not buildings that many other colleges would want, and he did not count into the square-foot costs a number of items that are normally included. In my opinion, other colleges can learn little about buildings from looking at Parsons. There were no secret formulas, no magic. There was just rock-bottom construction that grew out of economic necessity. Roberts did display a bit of magic, however, in rounding up his loans.

Did Parsons Make a Profit?

With these six ingredients making up the Parsons Plan, what did the college prove about the economics of higher education? Did Parsons in fact make a profit as Roberts claimed? No, Parsons never made a profit. But the answer to the first question is that Parsons probably did prove that a profit *could* be made by colleges under certain conditions, and that this college might itself have turned a profit ultimately if it had not fallen afoul of its regional accrediting association.

The Parsons Plan did produce for most of Roberts's regime a good deal more income than was required for the day-to-day operation of the college. Parsons did not have an operating deficit (as distinct from an overall, general deficit) for most of Roberts's administration. By the end of that administration, the college was indeed "making millions," as Roberts liked to claim, but not in the sense that most people would understand. To be specific, Table 2–2 shows the main revenues and expenditures of the college for the final two years of Roberts's administration.

As can be seen, the college had over $3 million in 1966 and over $2.5 million in 1967 that was "excess income." Between 1961 and 1967, the college generated about $9 million dollars in this kind of excess income. There were years in which

TABLE 2–2

Main Revenues and Expenditures of Parsons College, 1966–1967

MAIN SOURCES OF REVENUE	1966	1967
Tuition and fees from students	$7,457,114	$9,219,881
Auxiliary enterprises (mostly board and room)	5,316,115	6,170,390
Gifts	157,468	445,392
Other sources (including endowment)	254,294	242,851
	$13,184,991	$16,078,514

MAIN EXPENDITURES		
Instruction and educational administration	$3,877,089	$5,746,037
Scholarships and grants	868,897	1,532,149
Business and financial administration	1,003,229	1,294,687
Auxiliary enterprises (see above)	2,712,941	3,010,260
Operation of physical plant	632,081	863,334
Interest on loans	509,601	568,521
Other expenditures	374,585	503,130
	$9,978,493	$13,518,128

the excess income figure was inflated by the overevaluation of gifts of property that the college had received, but these instances do not alter the total pattern very much. So in the sense indicated above, the college did indeed make a "profit." A big one. And if colleges had to worry only about their operating expenses, Parsons might furnish an excellent example of how to meet those expenses and make money at the same time.

There are, no doubt, those who would quarrel with this suggestion, holding that even if Parsons did generate a lot of excess income, nothing much was proved because of the college's failure to carry on an instructional program of high quality. They might hold that Parsons would have had no such excess if it had done everything it said it was doing educationally, for that would have consumed all such funds. I would not agree with this assessment, though I would agree, as is clear by now, that Parsons certainly did fail to do all that it claimed. I think that Parsons did offer a reasonable quality of education as I will attempt to show, and that it *could* have fulfilled most of its claims and still have generated excess income. But what it really needed to do, of course, was to scale down its claims.

Unfortunately, colleges have to worry about more than operating costs. They do have to build buildings, and colleges that are expanding at a rapid rate have to find huge sums of money to finance buildings in advance of the arrival of each year's additional students. As I have said, Roberts raised an astonishing amount of money as loans for his building program, though never enough to finance all of the buildings that were needed. To make up the difference, he transferred most of his excess revenue to the "plant fund."

As a result of all this, Roberts built a campus with a high book value but one that was constantly in a financial bind. When he arrived at Parsons, the entire campus was worth perhaps $1 million; though one does not know what it would have brought if anyone had actually been interested in buying it, the figure would have been lower. But it also had a debt of $700,000. When Roberts left twelve years later, the campus had a book value of $21,433,554 and total assets of $22,231,-177. It also had total short-term and long-term debts to the tune of $14 million. One way of looking at these facts is to say that the value of the college had therefore increased by roughly $8 million during Roberts's regime. That $8 million had been transferred over the years out of excess income into the building program. Roberts added that to his loans in order to put up about $20 million worth of buildings. Of course, the campus was not "worth" $21 million or anything like it on the open market, but that is what had been pumped into it.

Although there was a continuous financial problem with buildings and recurrent financial problems of other kinds, they did not become critical until Parsons was disaccredited and suffered a precipitate decline in enrollment. In other words, Roberts for all his fiscal problems would probably have proved his theory if he had stayed out of trouble with the rest of the educational community. He would probably have demonstrated that a college following the main elements of the Parsons Plan could survive and prosper without gifts, endowment, or a yearly rattling of the cup among trustees and friends. He might even have proved, to the surprise and chagrin of most educators, that a college can make quite a lot of money. He would probably not have proved that schools can finance the necessary buildings on a pay-as-you-go basis out of current income, but he was not out to prove that. He was out to prove that current income could support interest payments on building loans and meet all the other operating expenses, including high salaries, at the same time. As things are, what he proved was probable success rather than actual success.

Surprisingly, Roberts was not really a good financial administrator, for there was a great deal of waste and mismanagement at Parsons. It was in spite of this operating inefficiency, not because of a supposed efficiency, that the college generated excess revenue. How much Parsons would have generated had Roberts run a tight ship is anyone's guess, but the figure would have been substantially higher. Raymond Gibson claims, on the basis of his experience as provost of the college, that $1 million could have been saved every year, with no curtailment of services, simply by lopping off the extravagant expenditures of the central administration and the athletic department; and adds that another $750,000 could have been saved by signing up faculty members on a year-round teaching schedule rather than giving them one-third of each year off with pay.[7] Robert W. Williams, vice president for business affairs at Parsons, explains the problem in this rather careful though hardly lucid fashion: "In the earlier years the account structure and the budgeting process reflected the management needs of the chief administrative officer [i.e., Roberts] as determined unilaterally by him."[8]

By any comparative measure, Parsons did have an expensive administration from the time Roberts took over. By his second year, the administrative budget of the college nearly equalled the instructional budget, an imbalance found in few institutions, and administrative costs continued to be exceedingly high throughout Roberts's regime. The administration grew top-heavy over the years although its members, apart from Roberts, changed with great rapidity. When Roberts arrived at Parsons, the chief administrators were the president and the dean of the college. By 1962 the college had a president, two vice presidents, an assistant to the president, and several deans. By the time Roberts left, there was a president, a provost, four vice presidents, four deans, and an assortment of minor administrators. The college was a growing institution, to be sure, but the administration seemed to grow faster than anything else.

Another former administrator at Parsons, now the business manager of another college, says that shortly after he arrived at Parsons he conducted a financial analysis of the place because he "could see that there was a lot of waste in personnel, a lot of waste in purchasing and expenditures, and the gist of the report that I did was really kind of blunt, I suppose."[11] Many old Parsons hands (as well as many students and some trustees) talk about financial abuses and petty graft that went on because of loose administrative procedures. According to one former high administrator, at one time, "there was complete bookkeeping chaos" that allowed a number of individuals to purloin college property, commandeer college automobiles or other equipment, and furnish parts of their homes at college expense. There is gossip to be heard on campus about federal tax evasion and a certain amount of hanky-panky by a few people associated with the school that went on with the college

credit cards (such as the charging of personal travel, entertainment expenses, and even clothing, to the college, or the
collecting of travel expenses twice). It is impossible to determine how accurate much of this gossip was. But what does
seem clear is that tight bookkeeping and day-to-day efficiency
were not part of the Parsons Plan. To the extent that the plan
succeeded, it did so in the face of waste and managerial shortcomings.

The Role of the Parsons Trustees

In the course of this book, the reader will no doubt ask himself about the whereabouts of the trustees of Parsons College.
Did they know what was happening at the college? Did they
know what kind of reputation the college was developing in
educational circles? Did they know how wide the gap was
between reality and the claims that were often made by the
college? This is perhaps the best place to deal with such questions since financial matters at any college consume most of
the time of the trustees, and financial policy was, after all,
the keystone of the Parsons College Plan.

To come to the heart of the matter at once, my opinion is
that the Parsons board of trustees as a body was often irre-
sponsible in governing the college. It yielded a fantastic
degree of authority to Roberts, far more than is true of any
other institution of my acquaintance. And in spite of many
warning signs, it failed to ask the right questions and to act
decisively at many critical points in Roberts's administration.
Yet one must recognize that the board's record differs only
in degree, not in kind, from that of many other boards of
trustees naturally composed, as they all are, of devoted, well-
meaning, very busy people who have many demands on their
time.

The Parsons board of trustees was heavily weighted in the customary way on the side of successful businessmen. It was a large board in relation to the size of the college. On Roberts's arrival, the board consisted of thirty-three persons, ten from Fairfield; there were four lawyers, four ministers, twenty-one businessmen, and four other professional people. The number of trustees climbed into the forties during Roberts's regime with the addition of businessmen from outside Iowa. When Roberts took over the college, twenty-five of the thirty-three trustees were from the state of Iowa and many of them, in Roberts's eyes, were ineffectual and a probable barrier to rapid change at Parsons. No fewer than nineteen of the trustees were "asked to resign" early in Roberts's administration, and all obliged. The board membership then shifted to out-of-staters until they formed a majority.

One of the comments made to me most often, both by trustees and by others, was that Roberts had the board in his pocket, that he dominated it and could isolate or fire any trustee who was too much in opposition. "I was the strongest of the trustees," Roberts said to me.

He dazzled the board with his financial reports, which seemed to show that Parsons was in excellent financial health and growing at a remarkable rate. "There was really no reason," wrote one dissenting trustee to another in 1963, "to have a board since Roberts has a completely free rein." Even when the trustees failed to approve one of his proposals, Roberts was often able to carry it out in some other manner. As long as the college seemed to be in such splendid financial shape, the trustees were not disposed to stand in his way.

Thus, permissiveness is perhaps the best word for the Parsons trustees. They might, for instance, turn down a Roberts proposal to buy a college jet for his travels, but would not veto his action when he leased one instead. Or they might not give him specific permission to buy and sell land but when he did so would fail to establish a strong policy against it.

Nor did the trustees require Roberts to get multiple bids from building contractors, which might have reduced the college's expenditures for buildings. Roberts frequently dealt with only one contractor. Neither did the trustees block the overvaluing of a hotel property that was given to the college in 1963 in exchange for a lifetime annuity to be paid to the donor. The trustees valued the property at $500,000, which amount was then entered on the books as income from gifts that year and entered so that it was included in the $1.5 million that the college claimed that year as "excess of income over current expenditures." The next year, however, prodded by its auditors, the college revalued the hotel and reduced it to $100,000, thereby reducing the income as recorded the previous year by $400,000. Nor did the trustees decline to allow the college to do business with a contracting firm in which a trustee had a large interest. Instead they agreed, at a time when the college was having trouble raising loan money, to a contract that called for the college to pay a finance charge of no less than $750,000 on a dormitory building program that itself cost $2,250,000, on which figure the college would also pay the normal interest rate. "We had the additional students already signed up," says C. Clyde Wright, then chairman of the board of trustees, "and we had to have dorms for them. It was the only way to get the financing. We had to get things done." Roberts admits that a serious conflict of interest could be said to exist in the matter but defends the $750,000 finance charge as unavoidable.

Roberts was even allowed to use Parsons funds to help start other colleges for which he also served as paid consultant. This aid from Parsons, which was estimated in 1967 by the Parsons auditors at over $500,000, took the form of paying the salaries of people from Parsons while they spent full time at the satellite colleges, sending the colleges some of Parsons's used furniture and other equipment, helping the satellites build library collections, and so on.

All of these activities were, to say the least, extraordinary and could have been permitted only by a board of extraordinary permissiveness. One of the college's financial consultants raised the question of whether the trustees might not have left themselves open to a charge of violating "the prudent man rule" that by tradition is supposed to govern the decisions of trustees of tax-exempt and public organizations. Still it would be wrong for one to think of Parsons's trustees as a wholly pliable body molded by Roberts. The majority of the board were undeniably permissive, but there were always some members who fought Roberts hard and at least a few who were always aware of the college's true financial condition. Two local trustees, John Hunt and Walter Williams, were of this group, though both eventually resigned from the board out of frustration.

Another trustee, W. W. McCallum, president of John Morrell and Company, and for some years head of the trustees' finance committee, tried as early as 1961 to enforce a tight administrative and financial policy on the college. At that time the college was approaching a financial crisis and seemed unable to meet current bills of about $600,000. McCallum worked out a plan of rescue in which the trustees put up collateral and the institution's creditors were given notes to be paid off over a number of years. But in subsequent years he was unable to enforce the tighter financial policy he had in mind and therefore resigned from the board. And there were others who resisted Roberts. There was James Camp, president of a savings and loan association in Des Moines; Richard Hoerner, for years the president of the board and one of its most dedicated trustees; and William Miller, a vice president of the American Oil Company. In addition, still others fought Roberts on one issue or another.

But as a body the Parsons board has much to answer for. When all the qualifications are made—that they were very busy men, that they had only limited access to accurate information, that they felt Roberts to be so successful in important matters that he should not be tried over minor ones, that they did resist singly on occasion—the fact remains that the trustees allowed Roberts an incredible degree of latitude. They must accept a large share of responsibility for the results.

There was, then, a goodly gap between theory and practice in the financial life of the college. Far from raising cost accounting to a precise science in educational administration, Parsons suffered from some monumental inefficiencies. Far from making a profit, the college was deeply in debt throughout Roberts's administration. Far from persuading people in higher education of the validity of its fiscal claims, Parsons has reinforced the natural conviction of educators that private colleges must have a continuous supply of gifts in order to survive.

Nevertheless, Parsons did demonstrate, for all the problems and abuses, that certain important things are possible in college finance. It demonstrated that a college *could*, whether or not one thinks this college *did*, so organize itself as to offer education of reasonable quality, pay its staff high salaries, and at the same time produce enough revenue to meet its full operating expenses. That is no mean achievement in view of the perilous condition of many of our private colleges and universities. It also demonstrated that a college so organized would, if well run, have an excellent chance of generating enough income to pay the interest on the loans it needs to put up buildings, and that it might therefore become entirely self-sufficient. At the very least, Parsons demonstrated that there are some financial alternatives to the present orthodoxy that are worth serious consideration by other institutions. The question is whether Parsons's current and professional reputation will block an honest evaluation by other colleges of the economics of the Parsons Plan.

Now it is appropriate that we examine in some detail the theory and the practice of the Parsons Plan as it unfolded in those few hectic years in the booming little college town of Fairfield, Iowa.

N O T E S

[1] Millard G. Roberts, "We Must Manage Our Total Educational Process," November 26, 1963. Italics in original.

[2] Millard G. Roberts, "Must Your College Lose Money Every Year?" August, 1962.

[3] Millard G. Roberts, "Do We Need More Community Colleges?" May, 1964.

[4] Millard G. Roberts, "Better Education for Less Money," undated.

[5] Ralph C. Hutchison, *A Study on the Utilization of Teaching Resources of Parsons College* (Philadelphia: United Presbyterian Board of Christian Education, 1960), Vol. I, Chap. 2, 4.

[6] Grayson Kirk, "College Shouldn't Take Four Years," *Saturday Evening Post* (March 26, 1960), pp. 108–111.

[7] Raymond Gibson, "The Scholarch of Parsons and the NCA," *Phi Delta Kappan* (June, 1968), p. 591.

[8] Robert Williams, *Institutional Profile*, 1968, p. 79.

3: The Name of the Game Is Students

> Over the amount of ability that we possess we have no control, for God has portioned out this mirror of the understanding, this inner eye, according to His will. But it lies in our power to prevent it from growing dusty and dim.
>
> —COMENIUS

> The great American dream is universal education. The great American tragedy is that education is confused with schooling.
>
> —WILLIAM GRAHAM SUMNER

> Education has really only one basic factor, a *sine qua non*—one must want it.
>
> —GEORGE EDWARD WOODBERRY

Throughout the industrialized world, admission to institutions of higher education is a strongly competitive matter governed by state-administered examinations. It is the central government in most countries that, through its conduct of the examination system, decides who will go to college. Even in countries such as England or Russia where the institutions control their own admissions, the main criterion is the performance of applicants on essay-type examinations that represent a national publicly recognized standard.

The United States is unique among the advanced nations in the manner in which institutions of higher education obtain their students. No other nation of the world admits anything

like the percentage of young people that we do or has anything like the number of institutions that we do relative to
population. Sometimes our state legislatures or other government bodies determine what the admissions policy of tax-
supported institutions will be. When they do, they use the
criterion of the student's rank in his high school graduating
class, with the exception of New York State which uses a
written examination. All the rest of our institutions—that is,
many tax-supported and all private colleges and universities
—make their own rules about who gets in and do their own
searching for students in the open market.

Institutions of higher education in other countries are mostly
state institutions whose facilities, dependent on tax funds, are
rarely adequate for the numbers of qualified students who want
in. Whereas the typical problem of an American student
headed for college is whether he will make it to the "college
of his choice," the problem for his counterpart in the rest of
the world is whether he will make it to college at all. Nor does
any other nation have anything like the dual system of private
and public institutions that we do, wherein most institutions
engage in the vigorous "recruitment" of students. The idea of
an institution's maintaining a staff of people to travel around
the country trying to persuade students (sometimes with the
help of high-pressure selling techniques) to sign up for their
institution would be incomprehensible in most of the world.

All this is another way of saying, as did Sir Michael Sadler
in 1921, a time when a far lower percentage of young people
went to college than do now, that higher education is "one of
the religions Americans believe in. It has its orthodoxy, its
pontiffs, its noble buildings. Education is the Established
Church of the United States." Since World War II, this
established church has undergone a massive expansion and a
fundamental change. We have moved steadily away from a
dual system of public and private institutions toward one in
which the tax-supported institutions are dominant. Although

we still have more private than public institutions of higher education, many of them are small and ailing and all of them together enroll fewer than half as many students as do the public institutions. This shift of students from private to public colleges seems certain to continue and in another decade will probably reduce enrollments in private institutions to perhaps one-third of what it is in public institutions.

The reasons for this shift need not detain us. The point is that private colleges in the United States, except for the best known, selective ones, are facing increasingly tough competition from public institutions for students, and many of them are probably not going to compete over the next ten or twenty years well enough to survive. Of course, all of them would like to have what there is not nearly enough of to go around: the good student willing to travel and able to pay. The low-ability student, even if he is willing to travel and able to pay, may stay home and go to a junior college or an unselective four-year public institution. The good student may be willing to travel but not able to pay; or if he is able to pay, will not settle for anything but a good college. At the same time, the good private colleges have been raising their admission standards along with their fees to the point that they have greatly narrowed the size of the group from which they can pick their students, thus driving many relatively good students into the public institutions.

By recording these facts, I mean only to pose a question for the reader. If you were Millard Roberts taking over Parsons College under the conditions that prevailed in 1955, where would you concentrate your efforts? On many things, no doubt. But you would have to give a very high priority to increasing enrollment. Without that increase, you would be hamstrung in everything else, particularly in financial matters. More than ever before, the name of the game in our private colleges—the game of survival—is students. Colleges like Parsons will survive only if they can become more efficient than private colleges usually are. And most institutions do what they have to do to survive.

How, then, would you increase enrollment at a college where traditionally the students came from the surrounding area and where competing institutions, both public and private and selective and nonselective, were available in quantity? You might say to yourself that you would set about creating special programs at Parsons that would distinguish the institution from others and give it something to sell. And indeed private colleges are going to have to do something like this if they are going to compete with each other and with public institutions. But instant programs of any worth are not possible. Good programs take years to develop and prove themselves; meanwhile you have a declining institution on your hands.

Or you might say to yourself that the college would have to follow the market and seek students where the chances of finding the greatest number of them were best. That decision would take you eastward to the seaboard, where the numbers of students who are able to pay and who have limited opportunities in their own states are highest. It would take you to such places as New Jersey, New York, Massachusetts, and Connecticut. Having got there, what would you have to sell? How would you persuade students from well-heeled eastern homes to travel to a small town in southeastern Iowa to attend a college that neither they nor their parents had ever heard of, or that they had indeed heard of but not in any reassuring fashion?

The Grinnells and Carletons of the Midwest can recruit widely and fill their classes with good students. But the harsh facts of life are that low-prestige colleges, having little to sell, do not attempt to recruit a thousand miles from home. If they decide to do so, their approach is dictated for them. If they cannot sell prestige, they must sell opportunity; if they cannot sell selectivity, they must sell receptivity; if they cannot sell enough freshmen, they must sell the drop-outs from other colleges. Whatever they do, they will naturally make a virtue of necessity. They will find intellectual arguments and emotional appeals to support decisions that they actually had to make in advance on hard, practical considerations.

The Open Door and the Second Chance

And so it was with Millard Roberts and Parsons College. Parsons was probably the only low-prestige college in the Midwest to have recruited large numbers of students from the eastern seaboard, although several other institutions are now following its example. Parsons did so and continues today to do so by the simple but controversial device of an "open-door" and a "second-chance" admissions policy, combined with highly organized and very aggressive recruiting. Roberts decided that the only way in which the college could significantly increase its enrollment in a short time was to let the world know that it stood ready to take almost any high school graduate and give him a chance, and that it stood ready to take most college drop-outs and give them a second chance.

In advertising itself as an institution that welcomed drop-outs and below-average freshmen Parsons was following an old, not a new, policy. It represented no philosophical change, for the college had always followed an open-door policy, as do most such colleges; and it had followed as much of a second-chance policy as the market allowed. The difference after 1955 was that the market allowed a great deal more, thanks to Roberts's promotional campaign, than had ever been available before.

Still, when such a policy is publicly proclaimed far and wide, instead of being followed discreetly in the fashion of many colleges, the institution must try to justify it. Parsons did so by talking a good deal about "salvaging" students, about those students who had finally caught intellectual fire at Parsons and had taken degrees, about the wash-outs from other institutions who had gone to Parsons and from there to graduate schools to earn Ph.D.'s, and in particular about the democratic right of all young people to have a try at a college that was interested in them. One can easily scoff at all this as rationalization, but it is supported by American traditions that are accepted more widely today than ever before. Many educators, administrators, and trustees defend the open door not merely because their institutions may have to follow such a policy to survive, but because they genuinely believe that everybody should have his chance; and also because they may believe that high grades in either high school or college are not very closely related to subsequent success in "life." One of Parsons's most active trustees remembers that early in Roberts's administration, "We made a survey of the trustees and found that eighty per cent had been C and D students in college and high school, and are now presidents and vice presidents of corporations and successful men."

A similar case, if couched in more euphemistic language, was made by Parsons itself in various documents. Typical of its defense of the open door and the second chance is this passage:

Parsons College recognizes that a student may have ability that has not been allowed to work for him because of a lack of direction; it also recognizes that some students need additional help in order to function effectively as students and citizens. Further it assumes it is possible for a student to perform poorly in high school or another college for a variety of reasons and yet do well when he is given a new opportunity under a system which emphasizes individual help.[1]

Or it found historical precedent in America's egalitarianism or in our tradition of offering refuge to the down-and-out from other nations:

> Parsons College is dedicated to the common man and does not apologize for that policy. It is committed to the idea of a second chance for the well motivated student . . . this nation was founded upon the idea of a second chance for millions who came to our shores. This institution is concerned about the previous achievements of those who come here, but it is more concerned with their potential—what they are capable of becoming.[2]

Or it suggested that the intellectual elitism of other institutions made them insular and was contrary to the Parsons philosophy, freely arrived at:

> The College eschews the provincialism and exclusiveness that can make a campus an artificial world. Parsons College, therefore, invites and accepts students from a great variety of backgrounds and from all parts of the country and world. We believe that every young person ought to have the opportunity to benefit from the kind of general and specialized education that Parsons offers. To this end, it is the policy of the College to encourage anyone with a high school diploma or its equivalent to apply for entrance.[3]

This philosophy, however, was transitional. Parsons was looking forward to the time when it could become selective, the goal of all second-rank colleges. When a college reaches the point that it can turn students *down*, it has reached the first step on the status ladder in American higher education. Parsons was no different in this aspiration from any other college, but meanwhile it had to make its case for non-selectivity.

Parsons also defended itself by pointing to the admissions policy of other institutions, with some justice as I have indicated. "All colleges," as an Eastern admissions officer remarked to me, "are open-door institutions about the fifteenth of August when they see how far short they may be of filling their beds." Then too, it was not so many years ago that our best known institutions were unselective. Until World War II, even the Amhersts and the Harvards of this world took almost anybody who applied and could pay, and only in recent years have moved to a position of turning away 80 per cent or more of their applicants.

Many of the colleges that were Parsons's worst enemies and in competition with it for students held the door open just as widely as Parsons, some even taking students not admissible to Parsons! Even a few of our well-known universities, such as Temple University in Philadelphia, have a long record of deliberately seeking out students with poor high school records and examination scores. In the 1940's there was one college in Iowa that advertised a policy of taking only students from the lowest quarter of their graduating class. The new Federal City College in Washington, D.C., has perhaps the least selective policy in the country. Its first class was chosen by lottery because of the surplus of applicants.

In 1968 the federal government appealed to institutions of higher education to take students from slums and poverty areas and to take veterans who might otherwise shun college, and to take them whatever their paper qualifications. At least one institution responded by recruiting students in neighborhood bars. Junior and community colleges are open-door institutions catering to many first-generation college students and offering them a mixed bag of liberal and vocational studies. Today colleges freely advertise in the national press with sales pitches like this one:

WE LOOK TO YOUR FUTURE . . . . NOT YOUR PAST

_____ College is dedicated to giving bright young men and women a chance for a successful college career . . . even if they haven't previously shown academic strength . . . in high school or early college years.

In other words, "If you are a college drop-out or if you have a poor record in high school, consider us because we want you."

It is still the case with a number, albeit a diminishing number, of state colleges and universities that any student who has a high school certificate or the equivalent is admitted. The typical practice is fairly brutal and extremely expensive for the taxpayers: the institution takes in a freshman class of two or three thousand students or more, puts them in large classes taught by graduate assistants, forces them into a set curriculum which they are expected to accept if they want to go to college, provides little if any personal help—and washes them out in tidal waves at the end of the first and second semesters.

I record all this to put Parsons's drive for students into a larger perspective. I do not mean to argue here the wisdom of open-door and the second-chance policies as such, though I would be quite willing to argue it. I would, that is, defend the record of America's institutions in accepting unpromising students, but that record seems to me to need no defense. Parsons, however, is not thereby provided with an excuse for some of the practices it followed in recruiting and retaining students. It did not invent the open door or the second chance, but it did promote them in some unorthodox ways.

Payment by the Head

Parsons, as I have said, made the recruitment of students the first priority and devoted a great deal of time and energy to it. Most of this effort was necessarily directed toward the recruiting of freshmen. Parsons sought transfer students and drop-outs as well, but had to rely mostly on general publicity and word of mouth to find them since no other institution was going to furnish Parsons with a list of its own drop-outs. Parsons maintained recruiting offices in Chicago and midtown Manhattan and developed a number of enterprising techniques for identifying likely students and getting them to Parsons. It had an admissions staff larger than that of most universities. At one time it had as many as nineteen recruiters in the field, compared to perhaps four or five that another institution of similar size might have.

Parsons paid these recruiters a base salary. Above that salary there was a bonus system through which the recruiter collected a payment from the college for every student that either sent in a paid application or actually enrolled. That is, a recruiter was paid by the head on two scales: he received one payment for each of his students who applied to Parsons and paid the application fee, and a second payment for each of these students who actually appeared on the campus and signed up. People sympathetic to such practices would call them nothing but old-fashioned incentives. People unsympathetic, and that would include most educators and probably all professional organizations, would call them unethical. I would count myself among the latter group, feeling that the abuses built into such a system are far more serious than are the undeniable problems of keeping recruiters on a salary only.

The most obvious abuse involved is pressuring the prospective student instead of counseling him. Recruiters from good colleges, one hopes, will as readily advise a student against applying to an institution as they will encourage him if they are convinced that their school is not the college for him. Their colleges can afford such a policy. Recruiters on a payment-by-the-head system, representing a college hungry for students, are apt to employ all kinds of hard-sell tactics to get the student enrolled. They might engage in anything from outright lies ("Yes, we have a program in Russian" or, "These new dorms will be finished by fall and you can have a room in them") to pressuring the student and his parents to get the application in immediately or face the possibility of being turned down later.

It is for such reasons that professional organizations rightly condemn bonus payments, for college admissions is one field in which parents have a touching if naïve faith untinged by a cautionary *caveat emptor*. Unfortunately there is no industry-wide code of ethics in college admissions and recruitment, but the Association of College Admissions Counselors, of which Parsons was a member until it was disaccredited, does publish a "Statement of Principles of Good Practice," which says in part:

> Admissions counselors should be scrupulously careful to present clear and accurate information concerning their own institutions and to avoid ambiguous, questionable, or false information about competing institutions.
>
> The admissions counselor is a professional member of an institution's staff and receives compensation on a fixed salary.

The ACAC tries to police its members for violation of this code, but that is no simple job, nor are there any set penalties.

Again, therefore, one should beware of condemning Parsons *in vacuo*. Although a great many parents as well as educators would be shocked to think that *any* American college paid its recruiter by the head, the fact is that a number do. How many is very difficult to determine, for such payments can easily be buried in the admissions budget and are hardly a popular topic of conversation among offending admissions officers. But I have explored the subject enough to know that a number of colleges, including overseas colleges recruiting in the United States, use such a system. Also, one ought at least to be able to understand the dilemma of many poor colleges needing students. They cannot afford to maintain a large staff of recruiters on salary alone. Small-college recruiters, to be frank, are of very mixed quality, and quite a number lack the incentive necessary for the hard work of getting students to go to an unselective college. If the college therefore maintains only a small admissions staff, it also gets few students. If it can get recruiters who respond to a pay-ment-by-the-head system, it might be accused of "headhunt-ing" or of regarding students only as a commodity, but it might get students. I think the practice should be condemned and other steps taken to solve the recruiting problem (there are some), but Parsons was not alone in resorting to such a system.

Nor was it alone in another practice equally open to abuse but seemingly more readily acceptable to the admissions in-dustry. That is the arrangements some colleges make with high school counselors. Parsons paid a lump sum, a sort of retainer, to some high school counselors to help in recruiting students—to screen vast rolls of names of potential students, to call students up and make appointments for Parsons recruiters, to plan a visiting schedule for the recruiters, and possibly to take an even more direct hand in advising students to go to Parsons. Such arrangements seem to me clear con-flicts of interest, not mere moonlighting. Other small colleges often pay high school counselors in this or a similar fashion. Some also hire outside consultants and even public relations professionals to do recruiting work.

Even good colleges make their subtle supplications to the high school counselors. A high school counselor these days can spend a large part of his life visiting prestige institutions, being entertained, and living and eating well at the institution's expense. The ostensible purpose of such visits is to acquaint the counselor with the general virtues and specific programs of the institutions to which they might want to send their students. The fact is that counselors develop favorites that may not be unrelated to the treatment they receive. Small colleges usually cannot compete on the entertainment circuit and may be driven to other methods.

College counseling is a fair-sized business in the United States. In addition to the multitude of counselors employed by individual high schools and colleges, there are at least three large nonprofit associations whose aim is to bring searching students and searching colleges together for a fee. There are also a number of corporate, profit-making enterprises with a similar mission. Then there are hundreds of private entrepreneurs who operate their own college counseling business and who come and go in large numbers. None of these persons or groups is subject to any kind of private or governmental accreditation, supervision, or licensing; and the field is therefore quite susceptible to buccaneering practices.

There was one unsavory procedure that probably was original with Parsons and that illustrates the kind of invention that is always in danger of coming out of an incentive system. For a time during Roberts's administration, certain deans and faculty advisers to students were also paid by the head, in this case for the number of students they managed to *keep* on the rolls. Part of their job was to "counsel" students who were in danger of dropping out of Parsons. They then collected a payment from the college for each of these students who decided to stay. This practice was complemented by still other inventions, which we will have occasion to look at in later chapters, aimed at keeping students on campus and paying their fees even when the institution could do little for them.

The Parsons Student Body

The astonishing success of Parsons's promotional and recruitment programs is best illustrated by Table 3–1, showing

TABLE 3–1

Enrollment at Parsons College, 1955–1966

FALL SEMESTER	ENROLLMENT	INCREASE OVER PREVIOUS FALL
1955	357	35%
1956	579	60%
1957	672	16%
1958	810	20%
1959	982	21%
1960	1,651	68%
1961	1,863	12%
1962	2,231	20%
1963	2,567	15%
1964	3,325	28%
1965	4,304	30%
1966	5,141	19%

the total enrollments for the fall semester of each year from the time of Roberts's arrival to his departure. I gathered these figures, like most of the statistics in this book, from a variety of sources that were frequently in conflict, though not on an important scale; the figures may not be precise but are probably close.

Parsons had a fourteen-fold increase in enrollment in twelve years, taking the institution from the small-college ranks to small-university size. To fuel this unprecedented growth, Parsons had to look to the East, and the result of course was a radical change in the geographical distribution of the student body. When Roberts arrived at Parsons, 85 per cent of the students were from Iowa; when he left, 6 per cent were from Iowa, and over half the student body came from the five Northeastern states of Connecticut, Massachusetts, New Jersey, New York, and Pennsylvania.

Much of this growth was made up of transfer students who had dropped out or flunked out of other colleges and who were limited in the institutions to which they could then go. State colleges and universities will not accept transfer students who are not readmissible to their former institutions. Neither will the better private institutions. Thus the flunk-outs from our institutions, as distinct from the drop-outs, must find a second or a third or a fourth educational home among lower-level private institutions. Transfer students during Roberts's administration fluctuated between a low of 22 per cent of the Parsons student body to a high of 43 per cent, which puts Parsons among the highest transfer colleges in the country.

As to the academic qualifications of students when they arrived at Parsons, one must settle for less precise and complete information than one would want. Since 1961 Parsons has been a member of the College Entrance Examination Board (the agency that sponsors the College Boards) and therefore has figures on this national standardized test for freshmen at Parsons; but such scores were not available for transfer students who had no College Board scores on their record when they arrived. Thus the SAT information, while incomplete, is fairly good. One should also remember that the student body did not remain static on such measures as the SAT but gradually improved over the years.

A generalization that would hold true throughout Roberts's

administration is that SAT figures for Parsons students are
concentrated in the middle and lower ranges of the 200–800
scale upon which these examinations are scored. The upper
range is consistently thin. In other words, the Parsons student
body, as judged by the SAT, is skewed toward the bottom
half of the national age group, a fact that is hardly surprising.
To be more specific, Table 3–2 shows the SAT average scores
for new students during the later years of Roberts's administration, when the trend was upward.

TABLE 3–2

Average SAT Scores of New Parsons Students, 1963–1966

NEW STUDENTS IN THE FALL OF	Parsons Students Average Scores		National Averages	
	VERBAL TEST	MATHEMATICS TEST	VERBAL	MATHEMATICS
1963	448	472		
1964	461	478		
1965	479	498		
1966	468	462	440	509

These fall enrollments put the best light on the matter inasmuch as SAT scores for students at Parsons decline between the fall and spring incoming classes and between spring
and summer. So the average SAT score for the entire Parsons
student body would be lower than these scores indicate. The
national averages, which I have listed above for purposes of
comparison, are based on scores made in 1960 by a representative national group of 3,537 high school students studied
by the Educational Testing Service who later entered college.
Each year about 38 per cent of all high school seniors take
the SAT exams; that constitutes the great majority of
graduates who go on to college. Thus a reasonable supposi-
tion is that seniors who do not take the SAT are poorer as a
group than those who do, which in turn means that the

average SAT score for Parsons would be lowered if we had such scores for the entire student body.

To look more specifically at a typical year, suppose we take the incoming freshmen in 1964. Out of a total of 566 freshmen that year, 380 (67 per cent) scored below 500 and 186 (33 per cent) above 500 on the SAT verbal test; and 333 (58 per cent) scored below and 233 (42 per cent) above 500 on the mathematics test. Looked at in still another way, 280 of these freshmen, just over half, were in the lowest two-fifths of their high school graduating class. It is not hard to find a number of other four-year colleges that require the SAT for admission and whose students have lower averages than these. Over half the entering class of some colleges who are members of the College Entrance Examination Board score below 400 on the SAT.

We can conclude then, that to the extent that we consider the SAT a fair measure of student ability, we may say that Parsons students during the later years of Roberts's administration compared reasonably well on verbal skills with the great mass of students who go on to colleges in the United States, and less well on mathematical skills. On the SAT measure alone, Parsons students would compare pretty well with those of a number of other American colleges.

Where, then, did the stories come from about the dismally low ability of Parsons students? Partly from Parsons itself— from former faculty and staff members; partly from the early and middle years of Roberts's administration, when the student body was of lower ability than in the later years. For example, one study published in 1963 by the former director of the student counseling bureau at Parsons found that as much as 60 per cent of the Parsons students from 1960–1962 had an IQ below 107, with significant numbers below 95. Looking only at the incoming freshmen, the report said: "A check at random of 489 freshmen admitted between summer 1960 and spring 1962 shows that

232 of them (47.4 per cent) had an IQ below 100 . . . . of this 489, there were 351 (71.9 per cent) with an IQ below 107."[4] These figures were based on an intelligence test given at Parsons in the late 1950's and early 1960's, which has since been discontinued.

It was during this same period, particularly after the fall semester of 1960 when the enrollment made an unusually large jump, that faculty members complained of having "real hoodlums" and "absolute bums" in their classes. The problems of some students during that period and probably later as well were more medical than educational. "I had students in class," says one experienced Parsons professor, "who were under such heavy sedation that they were uneducable." Thus from a low point in the early 1960's, the caliber of students at Parsons gradually rose until 1967, when it again declined because of the disaccreditation.

The claim was often made in Roberts's speeches and Parsons's literature that the college was following a one-third–one-third–one-third admissions program that was explained this way:

One third of each entering class is chosen from applicants from well-to-do families; one third from the middle class; and one-third from applicants who must earn their way. . . . One third of each entering class is admitted from Iowa and the states which bound it; one third from the area between the Appalachians and the Rocky Mountains; and one third from the east and west coastal areas or from overseas. . . . One third of the applicants are chosen from high school or preparatory school graduates who rank high on the College Entrance Examination Board tests; one third from those who rank in the middle grouping; and one third from those who rank in the lower third on the tests, or who have not been able to do successful work in other colleges or universities.[5]

This program was one of those *ex post facto* ideas dreamed up at Parsons to give a seeming rationale to practices that had grown haphazardly. Apart from whether such an admissions program makes any sense and would be feasible for any college, the fact is that Parsons never had such a program in any one of its dimensions. For most of Roberts's regime, the college took students wherever it could find them without worrying about elegant preordained patterns. The result was a student body that was heterogeneous in geography, fairly so in ability (more heterogeneous, for example, than the student bodies of prestige colleges), but rather homogeneous in certain of its disabilities, particularly in its apathy.

The Problem of Motivation

If one were looking for a single phrase with which to characterize Parsons students as a group, I suppose the lack of what educators call "motivation" would be it. It is a common problem in higher education but unusually so at Parsons, for reasons that are probably clear enough by now. In brief, Parsons was a school that sought out the students who had academic deficiencies; one of the main reasons for these deficiencies was lack of interest on the students' part in high school or a previous college; the students then brought their lack of interest to Parsons. So one of the college's intractable problems was how to fire academic interests in a very large part of the student body.

This lethargy seemed to carry over into other areas of student life. Parsons students led a very active social life but mostly on the party trail. Both dormitory groups and fraternities had "party houses" which they rented by the year away from the campus. But there were few social "activists" at Parsons and few groups interested in political reform. There were few student protests or demonstrations, and few groups interested in independent programs or inquiry. The campus newspaper, often run by scholarship students indebted to the administration, was poorly produced and uninteresting, though it carried many editorials about student cheating, the theft of examinations, and the lack of maturity of the students. Student interest in athletics was lively, and Parsons often fielded semi-professional teams made possible by the large number of athletic scholarships awarded by the college.

Parsons students also had money to distract them. Because of Parsons's eastern recruiting program and its search for drop-outs whose parents could pay the costs of sending their children away to an expensive college, it got a disproportionate number of affluent students. Many were older than their counterparts on other campuses and many were from *nouveaux riches* families without college traditions but with an emphasis on practicality and success. Many of the transfer students were able, having once been admitted to good colleges but having lacked the necessary interest or discipline to remain in them. Parsons therefore developed a reputation as a haven for lazy, rich, and frequently draft-dodging kids. This reputation was not lessened by the number of sports cars in the parking lots or the tales that got around (especially after a famous student riot in February, 1964) about the hard-drinking, drug-taking, partying, libidinous, hell-raising habits of the students.

Every college has its legends. At Parsons they talk about the student who shot up his dormitory with a machine gun; about girls who abandoned illegitimate babies on campus; about the student who rode around the town square, nude, on his motorcycle one midnight; about trunks thrown out of windows; dynamited buildings; cars deliberately demolished; general vandalism; about whole battalions of drunken students looking for kicks; and about the student who ran up a big bill at a local auto repair shop and whose father in New York told the complaining owner on the phone: "Give him all the credit he wants, but for God's sake don't send him home."

How much is true and how much apocryphal, I don't know, although it is a matter of record that at least one girl was indicted by a grand jury for manslaughter in the death of her illegitimate baby. Whether Parsons deserved its rock-bottom social reputation is not a question I can answer, and depends in part on what criteria one wants to apply. My own feeling is that the playboy element was larger at Parsons than at most schools of comparable size, but that it was somewhat short of what Parsons's dedicated enemies prefer to believe. The unbalanced ratio of males to females in the Parsons student body—there were always three or four men to every woman —probably had its effect on student behavior, especially since the ratio was not much relieved by the small town of Fairfield. The drug problem was severe at Parsons and the number of disturbed students, as distinct from the merely apathetic, seemed very large.

The problem of morale was to some extent inherent in the situation. Parsons was a college in the sticks that publicly advertised itself as a place for people with problems, and whose officers went around the country talking about saving "under achievers." That in itself would not be soothing balm to the self-respect of a prospective student. Then the student arrived on campus to find that the college had indeed collected a large number of people with various kinds of problems of anxiety, boredom, insecurity, and academic failure, and that the college did not act *in loco parentis* socially and only to a very limited extent educationally. Finally, the student became aware of the general reputation of the college in educational circles, and most of all he remembered the guffaws of friends and strangers when he told them he was a student at Parsons College. If a student did not have a motivational problem before he arrived at Parsons, he might easily develop one on campus.

Parsons knew it suffered from the lack of academic interest and the general apathy of a great many of its students. It tried to combat the problem by a variety of programs combined with lures, promises, threats, and heart-to-heart talks, and it tried to add some intellectual tone to the college by offering a number of generous "presidential scholarships," to better students. It met with some success, as we will see in Chapter 4, with many of the students who had been drawn in large numbers to Parsons by the college's promotional efforts. It also met with solid, unrelieved failure in its efforts with many. But first, we need to look at what it offered all of them in the way of an academic diet.

NOTES

[1] *Basic Institutional Data* (Parsons College, 1967).

[2] Raymond C. Gibson (provost of Parsons), in "Scholars Who Teach; a Profile of the Parsons College Faculty, 1966–67."

[3] *Basic Institutional Data* (Parsons College, 1968).

[4] Clarence J. Bakken, "High School Grades in Relation to College Success," mimeographed (February, 1963).

[5] The Parsons College *Bulletin*, 1963–1964, p. 11.

4: The Curtailed Curriculum at Parsons

> Among students, as well as among teachers, there has been a tendency to regard courses as something which exist in nature, instead of artificial simplifications for the mastery of what are complicated organisms, whether of nature or reason or society.
> —FELIX FRANKFURTER

> The number of courses offered by a college department is inversely proportional to the intellectual distinction of its faculty and the amount of basic knowledge in the field.
> —JOEL HILDEBRAND

> The good schoolmaster is known by the number of valuable subjects that he declines to teach.
> —SIR RICHARD LIVINGSTONE

The liberal arts college flourishes in the United States to an extent unknown elsewhere. The tradition it represents of broad post-secondary education is reflected in the degree requirements of practically all American institutions, thus giving special character to the undergraduate curriculum of the American college. By contrast, universities in Europe do not consider it their duty to be purveyors of broad, general education. They expect the secondary schools to look after that matter before moving students on to higher education. The program of studies at a typical English or European university is more specialized and restricted than at an American institution, with fewer lectures, no "discussion sections," much more independent work, and nothing that corresponds to the 120 semester hours, distributed neatly according to set patterns, that are thought of in our own institutions as certifying that a student is a bachelor of arts or sciences.

Because our colleges and universities take in such a high percentage of high school graduates, who span such a range of ability and background, the curriculum of an American college, like that of an American high school, looks like a smorgasbord. "Course proliferation" is a common term and a common worry, though there is far more debate about it than action. The problem is so pervasive among our colleges and universities that we ought to look at the general situation before considering Parsons's specific answer to it.

Ruml Revisited

Another peculiarity of our institutions of higher education is that the people who run them are guided by fairly definite and well-known criteria in everything but what is most important—the curriculum. Administrators have the recommendations of accrediting agencies, professional organizations, and special studies to tell them how to build buildings for a certain number of dollars a square foot, how to run the bookstore or the business office, how to make budgets, how to invest funds, how to negotiate with the government, how to treat the faculty, and how to do everything else except put together the educational program of the institution.

The absence of accepted guidelines for the making of a curriculum lets each institution go its own way untrammeled, with the result that most curriculums are simply a wide-ranging collection of unrelated courses reflecting no particular educational philosophy and certainly no great concern for economy. Only when an institution is in serious financial straits will a faculty or an administration be willing to submit the curriculum either to compulsory birth control so as to avoid ruin in the future, or radical surgery so as to avoid it in the present.

Nothing illustrates this endemic American phenomenon better than the debate that followed the publication a decade ago of a little book called *Memo to a College Trustee* (The Ruml Report), sponsored by the Fund for the Advancement of Education.[1] Most of it was written by Beardsley Ruml, a man with a career in both education and industry who was also known as the father of the American pay-as-you-go income tax plan. Ruml was a plain-spoken man of strong opinions. Some of his strongest opinions concerned the disabilities of college faculties and the irresponsibility of college trustees. The message of The Ruml Report was that college faculties had been allowed to usurp power over the curriculum, had then eloquently demonstrated their incompetence to exercise that power as a body, and that the time had come for college trustees to be bold and reclaim their lost authority. Having reclaimed it, they were advised to set about reconstructing the curriculum, acting through the administration, according to the economic facts of life. The number of courses should be greatly reduced, the size of classes at all levels should be increased, and a year-round plan of operation should be put into effect. Ruml had sent the first draft of his report to no fewer than one hundred distinguished educators and trustees and had got back a variety of commendations and condemnations.

After publication of The Ruml Report, its recommendations were debated in the popular and professional press. That discussion is still very timely, perhaps more so now than ten years ago, inasmuch as the basic problem of the proliferating curriculum is worse today than ever before. College professors as a group were displeased with Ruml, perhaps because, as one put it, "faculty attitudes toward the Ruml plan may be partly prejudiced by Mr. Ruml's attitude toward the faculty." *The New Republic* accused Ruml of trying to bring "Volkswagen production techniques" to education. An eminent college president commented that "You might as well put courses on videotape as to embark on a system of big lectures." Another president thought Ruml had "forgotten that a meat axe is most useful in a butcher shop, not in a college."

Some critics reacted to Ruml's plea for a curriculum based on solvency with highly idealized notions of what really happens in colleges. One professor, for example, wrote: "Course-cutters, like budget-cutters and surgeons, self-righteously get to feel that any and all excisions are pure gain; Ruml's is not the book to remind them that cuts are desperate remedies, that almost every curriculum limitation is also a limitation of the student's opportunities to be liberally educated."[2] Anyone who really believes that almost every limitation on the curriculum is a limitation on the student's chances for a liberal education moves in an academic world so different from that of Ruml and his sympathizers that no amount of discussion would bring them to agreement.

The Journal of Higher Education ran a symposium of responses to The Ruml Report. One contributor, who also regarded the central recommendation of the report as an infringement of the student's freedom, boggled at Ruml's assumption that the college might know better than the student what he should study:

The essence of the Ruml plan, despite his condemnation of "proliferation," is not so much to eliminate courses with small enrollment as to be dead sure that two-thirds of an individual's work is taken in courses that are as large as possible. If a student will adjust his ideas of a liberal education to what the college decides is best for him and most economical for the institution for two-thirds of his course program, then the college will let him have some real freedom of choice in respect to the other third.

Still another tried to state the case for liberal education as an attitude of mind rather than as an accumulation of knowledge, ignoring the obvious fact that it is both:

> The essential function of the college is not to secure mastery of a body of information, develop skill in mathematics or foreign language, or inculcate particular views on controversial questions. The function is rather to help students develop the attitudes and habits of mind that are the mark of the truly enlightened man or woman. In other words, the purpose of a liberal institution is to provide education; and as the old saw has it, "Education is what remains after one has forgotten everything he learned in college."

On the other hand, the well-known economist, Seymour Harris, came to Ruml's defense, saying that he was

> right in stressing the fact that the liberal college offers an excessive number of courses in its curriculum, and in pointing out that the widespread faith in the efficacy of the small class is misplaced. Study after study has shown that the results achieved in a large class are at least as good as those achieved in a small one. This is indicated by substantive as well as mechanical tests. Despite hundreds of experiments, faculties are unwilling to profit from the results of such tests.

A college dean commented:

The proliferation of courses is well recognized as a major evil in everybody else's world. It is an expensive evil, but it is an evil chiefly because students are allowed too early to sacrifice their experience of the excellent in order to participate in the special. The chief problem is that the privilege of talking on one's specialty is part of the psychological pay of the faculty.[3]

The chancellor of Syracuse University struck a particularly candid note which is perhaps even more valid ten years later:

In a college or university we don't have featherbedding for the sake of featherbedding—as is so often true in industry. Rather we have it because of custom, tradition, limited experience or conventional wisdom. The waste and inefficiency have never been systematically or scientifically examined. The truth is that we don't know as much as we think we do about our own business. And this goes for all of us—teachers, administrators, and trustees alike.

Because professors and administrators indeed do not know as much as they think they do about their own business, they can defend with equal passion curriculums that are in fundamental opposition to each other. They can hold, for example, as Robert Maynard Hutchins did at the University of Chicago in the 1930's, that a liberal education is best achieved with a core of perhaps a dozen courses, not with a potpourri of unsequential courses in which the element of free choice is the only discoverable principle. (Of course the faculties of some institutions nowadays strongly advocate a restricted curriculum also, but more in the interests of decreasing their own teaching loads than in the interests of the student or of institutional economy.) Other educators would hold to something approaching the opposite view: that a free choice of courses among a large number of offerings is the way to a liberal education. New York's City College, for instance, decided in 1968 to eliminate all but one required course in its undergraduate curriculum and substitute a wide range of choices for all students.

My own feeling is that The Ruml Report is still a useful guide to good fiscal and educational health for many colleges —though not for all, and not necessarily for those rich enough to maintain a high-quality smorgasbord. Parsons, not being rich, had to look to the reform of its curriculum.

The Parsons View of a Liberal Education

Parsons defined its institutional goals in the rather vacuous terms that colleges fall into when they talk about their purpose in life. Its broadly defined aims were to make students "appreciate the dignity and worth of all useful human endeavor . . . to recognize problems that need to be solved . . . to have an adequate knowledge of our cultural heritage," and so forth. Before Roberts's arrival, the college pursued these goals through a familiar combination of required courses in "general education" (in humanities, practical arts, science, and social science) and a large number of elective offerings, many of which were not actually taught for lack of enrollment.

Not much was done to prune the flowering curriculum at Parsons for the first few years of Roberts's administration, when the major effort was going into such matters as the recruitment of students. In fact Roberts expanded and inflated the courses offered in his early years until the church and other people began to question the size of the Parsons curriculum. But after The Ruml Report, change came fast. Richard N. Hoerner, then chairman of the board of trustees,

comments this way on the early years of Roberts's administration:

> You can't run a college with two or three hundred kids
> unless you have some kind of Santa Claus to keep it going.
> We needed more students but had nothing to sell. So I
> recommended, first, that we get some damned good advisers
> who could put together a program that would give us
> something to sell. And second, that all the trustees read
> that little dollar book [The Ruml Report].

Roberts therefore proceeded to get some advisers. Over a
period of time he used a procession of well-known consultants
in education, including such people as Ralph Cooper Hutchison, Algo D. Henderson, Theodore A. Distler, Raymond C.
Gibson, Earl J. McGrath, Hugh Stickler, Paul Reinert, Theodore McCarrell, and Lewis Mayhew. A number of such consultants made their first acquaintance with Parsons as
members of official visiting teams from the church or from
educational organizations and were subsequently hired by
Roberts as consultants. With their help Roberts did begin to
put together a program that would give Parsons something
to sell.

Hutchison, one of his first advisers, was the former president of Lafayette College and then head of an organization
called Studies in Higher Education, whose job was to analyze
the problems of small colleges and make blueprints for reform.
At the invitation of the Parsons trustees, Hutchison conducted a comprehensive study of the college in 1959–1960
and submitted a series of reports to the trustees setting forth
many recommendations that were accepted and adopted.
Central to Hutchison's proposals, as had also been true of
Ruml's, was the need for the trustees to exert authority and
strong leadership at the expense of many of the faculty's
traditional powers:

> The Board of Trustees, acting through a committee of the Board, carefully chosen and deeply dedicated, and under the leadership of the President, is . . . the only agency of sufficient strength to achieve the reorganization which will be necessary and to choose the curriculum to which the College must be limited.

Hutchison recommended a drastic reduction in course offerings, the creation of a mandatory two-year core curriculum, the adoption of a year-round trimester system of operation, high salaries and high teaching loads for the faculty, and a number of other measures that were subsequently taken up in whole or in part by Roberts and the trustees. To justify these radical changes, Hutchison offered the trustees a rationale that went beyond mere financial necessity, though that was certainly the preeminent concern. He offered them the tempting hypothesis that these changes would also produce superior education. With the blessings of the trustees, therefore, Roberts launched a major overhaul of the curriculum and of the academic calendar in 1960–1961.

The only important change before that time had been an ambitious "Great Books Program" that had started in the fall of 1958. The idea had been to require all students at the college to read a book a month throughout their Parsons career, the total number of books adding up to thirty-two. Lectures, discussions, and examinations were to accompany each book, and one hour of credit was to be given each semester. It did not work well. It was converted in the fall of 1960 to a series of three-hour courses. Then it was abandoned entirely as problems multiplied. One of the main problems was superficiality—a familiar companion of great books pedagogy and general education courses.

Other curricular variations came and went throughout Roberts's regime. There was, in fact, a tireless tinkering with the curriculum that made life difficult for the Parsons faculty and that is habitual among American colleges and universities. A recent national committee sponsored by the Hazen Foundation offers this abrasive comment:

> One of the great indoor sports of American faculties is fiddling with the curriculum. The faculty can engage in interminable arguments during years of committee meetings about depth versus breadth. They can fight almost without end about whether education should be providing useful or liberal knowledge. They can write learned books and articles about the difficulties of integrating human knowledge at the time of a knowledge explosion. And of course the battle between general and special education is likely to go on until the end of time. Curricula are constantly being changed. New courses are introduced, new programs are offered, new departments are created (to quickly become powerful vested interests of their own), sequences of courses are rearranged, honors programs are introduced, catalogues are rewritten, teaching loads are adjusted, and a grand and glorious time is had by all.
>
> The harsh truth is that all this activity is generally a waste of time as far as providing better education for students is concerned.[5]

Most educators would not accept this judgment, though they might admit that it has enough truth to be embarrassing.

Despite the constant tinkering, the Parsons curriculum did stabilize after the reconstruction of 1961 and remained substantially the same thereafter. It consisted, first, of a "core curriculum" that was mandatory for two full years and admitted of practically no choice. Students who came to Parsons as freshmen spent at least their first two years in this core, and a great many transfer students spent considerable time in it as well. Then, beginning in their third year, students could concentrate in one of perhaps twenty major fields, each of which was also sharply limited in the number of courses available.

Table 4–1 shows what the core curriculum looked like.

TABLE 4–1

Core Curriculum

SUBJECT	SEMESTER HOURS
Humanities (ancient and medieval worlds, renaissance, philosophy, fine arts)	18
Language (rhetoric, speech, one foreign language)	15
Social Science (history, political science, economics, psychology or sociology)	12
Science (biology, physical science, math)	15

That kind of two-year core is nothing new in American colleges, though it is much more prescriptive than most. A recent study of the catalogues of 332 colleges and universities indicates that the "general education" requirements for the bachelor's degree have changed very little over the last decade and that they add up to about 37 per cent of the total requirements for the degree,[6] as compared to 50 per cent at Parsons. All of the core courses at Parsons were offered every semester when there was adequate demand for them, so that students, whether freshmen or transfers, could make their way through the college at their own speed. It was always a point of emphasis with Roberts that the Parsons curriculum, by being so restricted and, so to speak, available, was an "ungraded" program that allowed every student to advance according to his ability and application, and to graduate not with his "class" but whenever he reached the end of the line.

Such a large and inelastic core curriculum represents one way of dealing with below-average students. Because many such students are academically and personally "lost," a core curriculum consisting of many survey courses gives them a chance to find themselves and identify their own interests and talents. A similar curriculum is found in Boston University's College of Basic Studies, a two-year administrative unit within the university with its own faculty and student body which is designed for below-average students. The college refers to its faculty as one with a "willingness to experiment" and one that "attempts to reach the students at all appropriate levels." The college readily acknowledges in its catalogue that it does not believe in an elective system for such students: "The College accepts the responsibility for determining what kind of general education the student will acquire rather than leaving this to chance gleanings from discrete and often unrelated courses of study."

Two assumptions are behind this approach to higher education, an approach that can be found in a number of institutions. First, that below-average students are so deficient in general liberal education that they must spend two years correcting that deficiency before moving on to other things; and second, that such students are better off working in a set, stipulated curriculum than in one with a lot of electives. A strong and persuasive case can be made for this theory.

Most institutions, however, particularly junior and community colleges, follow a different theory, or at least a different practice. They offer great freedom to the below-average student. On the theory that what he needs to do is shop around, he is invited to choose among many courses in many fields, academic and vocational. He is often required to take certain basic courses but nothing as comprehensive as was attempted at Parsons. There are institutions, ranging in prominence from Franconia College to Harvard, which permit their students to play a role in constructing some of their courses themselves—the ultimate extension of the elective system.

Although my own bias is toward a stipulated curriculum, particularly for below-average students, I do not propose any prolonged examination of old arguments about the elective system or about curricular freedom versus restriction. Both systems may "work," given a number of conditions. One of the conditions is the amount of money available. If a college lacks money, a large dictated core curriculum such as Parsons developed is entirely defensible on both financial and academic grounds.

The "upper division" curriculum at Parsons was much more orthodox in the way it was taught than the core that took up the first two years. However, tight controls were kept on the number of courses even in the upper two years. Roberts insisted that eight courses were ample for a major in almost any college department in any given semester, and he therefore restricted most departments to that number. He reasoned that an undergraduate would normally take only forty courses in his whole college career. If half of them were in the compulsory core, he would then need twenty upper division courses, not all of them in the same department. If most departments were limited to eight courses in any trimester, in contrast to most American institutions where the average is probably fifteen or twenty, they could still offer an ample range of work over the four trimesters that an undergraduate might spend in the upper division to satisfy the needs of a major.

From 1961–1967 Parsons offered a major in most of the customary liberal arts subjects and in various subdivisions of them. In addition the college tried other subjects from time to time, often without success. Parsons tried a major in home economics for a while but abandoned it, as it also did programs in nursing, journalism, industrial arts, and secretarial science. Off and on in an attempt to increase Catholic enrollment, the college even offered special courses for Catholic students in such subjects as the sacraments, grace and prayer, and courtship and marriage. The only nonacademic major, apart from elementary education and physical education, that drew students in large numbers at Parsons was business—which consistently had the greatest number of students of any department of the college.

Roberts made a point of saying that because every upper-division course was considered part of that department's major, students taking advanced courses outside their own major could not pick and choose among "mickey-mouse" offerings of the sort that abound in many colleges; they were limited, in whatever subject they took an upper-division course in, to one that was basic to a major in that field. Hutchison had recommended that the college limit to seven or eight the subjects in which it offered majors and that it add others only when they could demonstrably pay for themselves. Instead Roberts allowed the ordinary collection of majors, even when enrollment in upper-division courses was low. In other words, the upper division of Parsons College always included some courses that were quite small and that violated the economic principles upon which the institution was supposed to operate.

In their content, neither the lower- nor the upper-division courses at Parsons broke with orthodoxy, in contrast to what one might expect at an experimental college. No new paths were explored in regard to the substance of a liberal education, for the Parsons curriculum was quite conventional. In a word, the Parsons experiment was one in how to do more economically the job that liberal arts colleges usually do.

Classes in the lower division, the core curriculum, were often made up of two hundred or more students and were rarely below one hundred. These were the bread-and-butter courses of the college, the place where the economics of the plan worked best. It was the lower division that financially carried the upper division as well as other operations of the colleges. Courses in the upper division could also be large, enrolling sometimes from fifty to ninety students, but the average was much lower.

Just how many courses were offered in the whole college

in any given trimester is an elusive figure. It was never the same as the number in the catalogue (nor is it at most colleges). The Parsons catalogue always listed many more courses than were given, and never included all of those that were actually taught. Before the curricular reorganization at Parsons, Hutchison had found this situation:

> In company with most colleges of similar heritage, Parsons offers a selection of courses that might grace the catalogue of a much larger college or even a small university. . . . The 1960–61 catalogue carries the announcement of some 505 different semester courses in some twenty major fields. Furthermore, an additional 66 courses were scheduled and being taught but which are not included with those listed in the catalogue. Some of the courses seem to be "window dressing." The total number of courses scheduled the first semester was 150; the second semester was 153. Of the courses presumed available, 256 were not scheduled. Of all the twenty majors offered, seven were not elected by any-one in the class which graduated in 1960, two were elected by only one student each, three were elected by only two students each, and two were elected by only six students each. There were fewer than eight students in each of seven majors. To put it another way, more than eight students were enrolled in each of only six majors.[7]

After Parsons adopted the core curriculum and threw tight limits around the number of courses in the upper division, the college settled down to a pattern of actually teaching 60 or 70 per cent of the courses offered in the catalogue. Parsons continued to describe in its catalogue about 250 courses, a number of which represented "same as" or multiple listings, as being available, but it actually offered between 150 and 200, depending on the semester. During the last trimester that Roberts was on campus, 199 courses were scheduled for

4,859 students. In any event, one should remember that the big curricular reductions made at Parsons were carried out at the same time that the enrollment was steadily climbing. More important than Roberts's initial surgery on the Parsons course offerings was his refusal to add new courses as he added new students. By 1967 Parsons was probably giving fewer courses in relation to the size of its student body than any but a handful of special American institutions.

The Teachers of Parsons College

To man its large classes in the lower division and at the same time avoid the problems of pedagogy and morale that are associated with mass lecturing, Parsons strove to develop a faculty that was primarily interested in teaching and to combine it with other kinds of instructors to make up what Roberts rather pompously called a system of "team teaching." The problem facing Roberts, in other words, was how to give below-average students the kind of personal attention they presumably need when the college's finances made large lectures necessary. He tried to solve the problem in part by making the most of the big lectures of the core curriculum. He stressed the importance of good teaching and insisted that faculty members make teaching, not research, their main business. And in part he tried over time to solve it by developing a three-level hierarchy in the teaching staff, the top level of which he called the ranked faculty, most of whose number had the Ph.D. degree and who did the lecturing at Parsons. The second level was made up of preceptors (originally called associates) most of whom had the master's degree and whose job was to teach students in smaller discussion sections. The lowest level was made up of tutors with bachelor's degrees who taught students individually. The result, said Roberts, was team teaching.

Before Roberts developed this system, he had continued with a system of workshops that had been in effect when he arrived at Parsons, but with many changes. As the name suggests, workshops were a variation on the orthodox discussion sections that in most institutions are the principal form of undergraduate teaching, but at Parsons they came to be aimed particularly at the poor students and were taught by both the course instructors and associates who, having a master's degree, were considered below the faculty. As with most of Parsons's experiments, the workshops suffered from rigidity and from Roberts's assumption that any experiment was applicable to all subjects equally. Even more serious was the difficulty of getting the very students who most needed the workshops to attend them. A study done in 1960–1962 indicated that the workshops were of very little help to the poor students.

The workshops were dropped in the spring of 1963, when multisection courses were abandoned and large lectures begun, and a somewhat different kind of discussion section was established. The new discussion sections were conducted by the associates, a name that was later changed to preceptors when Parsons began to hire people for this specific job. The purpose of the new discussion sections was to review and repeat the material of the lectures with groups of twenty to forty students, making room for questions and discussion not possible in the lectures. Preceptors were supposed to be people working toward their doctorates, but Roberts paid them so well that he attracted a number of high school teachers with master's degrees who were quite willing to make a career of preceptoring at Parsons, thus weakening the claim sometimes made that team teaching was a new method of training future scholars and professors. Unfortunately these discussion sections never worked as well as the theory said they should or the administration said they did. They suffered from the limitations on subject matter imposed by the ranked faculty, from poor attendance by weak students who needed them, from the fact that some students would have heard the lecture upon which the discussion was supposed to be based and some would not, and from a lack of coordination with the lectures and lecturers. A further problem was created by the size of the discussion sections, which often had thirty-five to forty students in them and became particularly unwieldy in such subjects as foreign languages and English composition.

The third component of the Parsons system of team teaching, the tutorial program, began in 1963 and continued to expand for the rest of Roberts's administration. In theory the tutorial is where the Parsons students, the poor ones especially, got individual attention for their academic problems. They were supposed to meet with a tutor once a week in each of the core courses in which they were doing poorly and with his help grapple with their personal learning difficulties. Some tutors of a "warm" personality worked very hard and saw a great many students; some were "cold" and saw few. Some were highly effective with some students; some were rarely effective with any. All of them suffered to one degree or another from Parsons's intractable problem: how to get the poor students to attend. In short, the tutorials, like the discussion sections and the whole team teaching idea, must be considered an experiment that points to interesting possibilities but to no firm conclusions. (Success, however, did smile constantly on the tutorial program in one respect. It was an excellent device for recruiting students. It had a natural appeal to parents whose children were in academic trouble, and the Parsons recruiters made the most of it.)

The team teaching system exacerbated an already existing in balance in the teaching staff, in that it made an already top-heavy ranked faculty even more so. Because so much of the teaching work was done by lower-echelon persons who would normally occupy the instructor and assistant professor ranks in other colleges, these ranks were sparsely populated at Parsons. In the fall of 1966, for example, 102 persons out of a faculty of 116 were full or associate professors, meaning that only 14 persons occupied the junior ranks of instructors and assistant professors. Below the ranked faculty, however, were 83 preceptors and 58 tutors. By creating this three-level hierarchy in which the top level was limited as much as possible to Ph.D.'s and called the ranked faculty, Parsons could claim that the percentage of Ph.D.'s on its faculty was extraordinarily high. Roberts made this claim frequently, as did his senior administrators.[8] This too was a highly saleable item to parents and students and to uninformed people in the academic world. Eventually the college was forced to add its preceptors to the ranked faculty for purposes of arriving at the percentage of Ph.D.'s on the staff, thus lowering that percentage a good deal but still keeping it higher than that of most independent colleges and many universities.

What happened to the Parsons teaching staff under Roberts's administration is illustrated very simply by Table 4–2. Thus the student-teacher ratio, a favorite but misleading

TABLE 4–2

Degrees of Parsons Teaching Staff, 1955 and 1966

	FALL, *1955*	FALL, *1966*
Ph.D's on the staff	6	98
M.A.'s on the staff	16	98
B.A.'s on the staff	9	59
	31	255

measure used by accreditors and other people to judge the quality of an institution, would be very high at Parsons if only the ranked faculty were included but would be near the national average if all three classes of teachers were included. In the fall of 1966 when the enrollment was 5,141 the student-teacher ratio was slightly over 20–1 if we include all three classes of teachers at Parsons into the calculation, but it would be over 50–1 if we include only the ranked faculty. The most recent figure available for the national average is slightly over 18–1.[9]

The number of Ph.D.'s on the Parsons staff in relation to the number of students enrolled was about the same before Roberts's administration as during it. The difference, of course, was that they taught many more students under Roberts. The Ph.D.'s did almost all of the lecturing in almost all of the classes at Parsons. Roberts with some justice made much of this fact, for there are very few colleges or universities, no matter what their resources, that can claim to put the holder of a Ph.D. before every class in the institution, including the lowliest freshmen classes.

A good many classes in most institutions, whether small impoverished colleges or large state universities, are taught by instructors with a bachelor's or master's degree who sometimes are not far ahead of their students. Insufficient contact with scholars and senior professors is, as everybody knows, one of the principal grievances of American students, and perhaps one of the most valid. While many students at Parsons also lacked such contact because of the large lectures, they at least could count on a well-qualified professor in every course. No one would argue—certainly I would not—that a Ph.D. always makes a man a good teacher or that good teachers are all Ph.D.'s. Far from it. But when we are talking about people in large groups and general trends among institutions, it is surely clear that the ratio of Ph.D.'s to non-Ph.D.'s has an important bearing on the overall quality of an institution.

Who then were the Ph.D.'s that went to Parsons to compose the ranked faculty of which so much was made? They might be characterized as well-qualified but with some exceptions not well-known or outstanding people. One reason that they were relatively unknown may be that they were not researchers with a lot of professional publishing to their credit. A dedicated researcher would not be tempted, even by a high salary, to settle in a small nondescript college without graduate students and some distance from adequate library facilities. Thus most of the professors whom Roberts hired were people with degrees from respectable though not leading institutions. "They were what I call in-between people," says one man who knew the college well and who is himself a distinguished professor at a major university, "and they were good people for an independent college, but I would never hire them for my own institution."

They came in part for money, to be sure, for Roberts paid his faculty extremely well. Whether the faculty as a group had a greater interest in money than the faculties of other institutions is not a question that can be answered except by conjecture. The conjecture of many people is that they did. I confess the thought crossed my own mind when, fairly early in my study of Parsons, I received what might be called a financially inspired response from a former leading Parsons administrator laying down the conditions under which he would be willing to discuss Parsons College with me: he demanded a signed contract engaging him as a consultant at the rate of $100 an hour or $500 for an eight-hour day for whatever discussions we carried on, plus the right to veto any statements that I might attribute to him. (I decided the study would have to go forward without his help.) Whatever their reasons for going to Parsons, I believe that many if not most of the senior people involved would admit to having been overpaid, or at least paid well above what they could command at any other institution.

That some went with misgivings is demonstrated by the fact that they went on leaves of absence from their former institutions, a protective measure that is uncommon when one is changing jobs. And they left Parsons in uncommon numbers. The turnover rate of both faculty members and administrators at Parsons was far higher than at most institutions. "We should have a revolving door," said one Parsons administrator, "to facilitate the simultaneous exit and arrival of faculty members." Some left for fear of their own future (more than a few were soon afraid that they had committed professional suicide by going to Parsons in the first place); some left because they got caught in one purge or another; some left out of simple disillusionment and some got out, or were got out of the way by going to the satellite colleges. So great was the turnover of faculty members that an accrediting team visiting the campus in February, 1967, a few months before Roberts was fired, found only thirteen ranked faculty members who had been at the college as long as five years.

Then too, there were professors who wanted to leave but couldn't, who had become accustomed to the high salaries and who had irrecoverable investments in expensive homes in Fairfield. And some of course could not get jobs elsewhere even if they were willing to move. As a former senior administrator of the college said to me:

One poor man on the faculty had a lot of kids and a salary that was double or triple anything he had known before. It was the first time in his life that his kids had eaten well. He wanted to leave badly but couldn't. I remember Roberts telling me once that there were a number of people that would not leave and could not leave no matter what.

But the harsh judgments about the Parsons faculty that one can easily gather from talking to people should be applied with caution. With a few exceptions, the members of the faculty were not published scholars or eminent people with impressive backgrounds, but they were far better qualified as a group than the faculties of most four-year colleges in the

United States. And at least some of them were devoted teachers very serious about the idea that their main job was to teach students as well as they possibly could.

How well the students of Parsons College were in fact taught and what the general quality of a Parsons education was are central questions to which we now turn.

NOTES

[1] Beardsley Ruml, *Memo to a College Trustee* (New York: McGraw-Hill, 1959).

[2] Paul Lauter, "Memo from a College Teacher," *The New Leader* (Nov. 16, 1959), p. 22.

[3] See *The Journal of Higher Education* (November, 1959).

[4] William P. Tolley, "President's Bulletin Board" (Syracuse University, December, 1959).

[5] *The Student in Higher Education* (Hazen Foundation, 1968), p. 35.

[6] Paul L. Dressel and Francis H. DeLisle, *Undergraduate Curriculum Trends* (Washington, D.C.: American Council on Education, 1969), p. 30.

[7] Ralph C. Hutchison, *A Study on the Utilization of Teaching Resources at Parsons College* (Philadelphia: United Presbyterian Board of Christian Education, 1960), I, Chap. 4, 1.

[8] For example, William Munson, as Vice President for Academic Affairs at Parsons, says in one of Parsons's major pieces of sales literature that the Ph.D. degree is held by "more than 90 percent of the professional staff." See "Scholars Who Teach; A Profile of the Parsons College Faculty, 1966–67."

[9] "Preliminary Report of Student-Faculty Ratios in Higher Education, 1968–69," Institute of Higher Education, University of Georgia, mimeographed (June, 1969).

5: The Quality of a Parsons Education

The art of teaching consists in large part of interesting people in things that ought to interest them, but do not.
—ROBERT MAYNARD HUTCHINS

The courses I offer are Whitehead I, Whitehead II, and Whitehead III.
—ALFRED NORTH WHITEHEAD

Lessons are not given, they are taken.
—CESARE PAVESE

Somewhere in his writings, James Thurber describes a chance encounter he once had on the street with a friend, during which the friend asks, "And how's your wife?" To which Thurber replies, "Compared to what?" One needs to grapple with Thurber's question in judging the quality of a Parsons education, as well as in making most other judgments about the college. Nothing is easier than to make Parsons look bad by comparing it to institutions, practices, or standards that are not comparable. No other institution in the country was quite like Parsons, excepting possibly some of the so-called satellite schools. Although many other colleges were as "unselective" as Parsons, none took in the same kind of student body and none tried to do the particular job of retrieval and rehabilitation that Parsons carved out for itself. Because that job involved students who could afford to pay for the chance to improve upon their previous academic records, Parsons had few disadvantaged students. It did have a higher percentage of Negro students during Roberts's administration than a great many private colleges, and also a respectable number of scholarship students, but most such students were middle-class. Parsons was not a college that sought out the disadvantaged (nor did most private colleges at the time) and the apathy of its students was caused by factors other than a deprived home background.

While comparisons can be made readily enough in themselves between the standards of Parsons and those of other schools, judgments based on these comparisons, if they are to be fair, are not easy. Yet they must be made. To do so, suppose we look at those elements of the academic program at Parsons that are generally thought of in higher education as having the greatest influence on the quality of an institution.

The Attrition and Retention of Students

Earlier I described the kind of student body attracted to Parsons and the influence this inevitably had on everything about the institution. Important also to the quality of education offered at Parsons was the rate at which these students dropped out or survived. Both the attrition and retention of students at Parsons were high, a fact that is not as contradictory as it may seem. Attrition is the rate at which students leave a school for any reason before graduation. One would expect this rate to be high at Parsons, and it was. Retention is less a rate than a policy through which are defined the standards, mostly measured by grades, that students must meet in order to remain in good standing in the institution. Parsons followed a very loose retention policy in order to keep as many students as possible on campus. Therefore its retention was also high in that it retained a great many students who would have been dismissed by other institutions.

The attrition rate fluctuated, of course, over the years of Roberts's administration, more so perhaps than is true of most institutions. One study by a Parsons administrator found that over 70 per cent of the students who had entered Parsons in the fall of 1960 had left the college by the end of their second year.[1] A later study covering a longer span of time contained separate attrition data for students who entered Parsons as freshmen and those who entered as transfer students. One should remember that transfer students always made up an unusually high proportion of the Parsons student body, sometimes as high as 43 per cent and never lower than 22 per cent. For the students who entered Parsons as freshmen between 1955 (the year of Roberts's arrival) and 1962, the attrition rate—the percentage of those who *failed* to graduate—fluctuated between a low of 55 per cent and a high of 80 per cent. In other words, the college in its best year graduated 45 per cent of those it had taken in as freshmen and in its worst year only 20 per cent.

Transfer students did consistently better, perhaps because their native ability may have been higher, having been sufficient in many cases to get them into good institutions prior to their transfer to Parsons. Their attrition rate at Parsons for the same period of time fluctuated between a low of 27 per cent and a high of 49 per cent; meaning that in the best year Parsons graduated 73 per cent of the students it had taken in as drop-outs or transfers from other institutions, and in its worst year had graduated 51 per cent.[2] Another study lumped all students together and suggested that Parsons normally graduated a little less than 38 per cent of all the students it admitted,[3] freshmen and transfers, thus giving the college an overall attrition rate of 62 per cent. Still another calculation, this time for the single graduating class of June, 1966, indicated that 33 per cent of these graduates had entered Parsons as freshmen. The foregoing attrition figures are not precise but are sufficiently accurate to yield a general picture.

Nor can we be precise in comparing the attrition rate at Parsons with that of other types of institutions. Such statistics are neither plentiful nor particularly reliable. One of the better national studies of attrition was based on a sample of students who entered college as freshmen in 1961 at 248 institutions. The study sought to determine, that is, what had happened to these students four years later. Based on returned questionnaires, the investigators estimated that 65 per cent of the students in the sample had completed four years of college, though not necessarily a degree, by 1965 and that our national attrition rate was therefore about 35 per cent.[4] Presumably the national rate would have been estimated at a somewhat higher figure if the study had been limited to students who actually took a degree. A study of the senior colleges that make up the City University of New York (Brooklyn, City, Hunter, and Queens) found that while only 48 per cent of the students at these institutions took their degrees in the normal four-year period, 70 per cent took them within seven years of their original matriculation.[5]

If we therefore assume a national attrition rate for all institutions taken together of 35–40 per cent, Parsons would seem to compare badly. But the comparison is not very satisfactory because of the unique character of Parsons and because the above rate lumps all types of institutions together, some with exceedingly low attrition rates and some exceedingly high. The Parsons rate of, say, 60–70 per cent would probably compare well enough with the attrition rates of many tax-supported institutions, particularly some of the large state universities, but obviously not with the good private colleges. How it would compare with private colleges below the top level, I do not know, for no reliable figures for this kind of institution are available.

Millard George Roberts, the flamboyant and controversial president
of Parsons College, 1955–1967.

Parsons College, as this sign outside the railroad depot in the town of Fairfield, Iowa suggests, is by far the largest industry in town.

The town square of quiet, prosperous, conservative Fairfield. For most of Roberts's administration, Parsons brought unprecedented amounts of money into the town, together with congestion, local inflation, and a great many Eastern students who often complicated town-gown relations.

A view of the older and pleasanter part of the Parsons campus. The building in the center-right is the oldest at the college, having been built as a private residence in 1854.

One of the student dormitories at Parsons. "Motel modern," it was dubbed by the students, who did not share Roberts's enthusiasm for plain, low-cost construction.

A view of part of a new institution, Hiram Scott College, at Scottsbluff, Nebraska—the healthiest of the six "satellite" colleges that
Roberts nursed into being. Five of them are left and are now wholly
autonomous.

The attrition question is further complicated by the fact that a great many students who drop out of one or more institutions become part of the attrition rate of their previous institutions but go on to complete a degree somewhere else. Many students left Parsons for reasons other than academic failure and went on to other institutions and sometimes back to their old one. Also, as I have said, one would *expect* a college like Parsons to have a high attrition rate, but what does one compare that rate against in order to decide if it is good or bad? About all we can say is that the attrition rate at Parsons for both transfer students and those who started as freshmen was much higher than the national average but probably not much higher than that of a good number of public and private institutions. That still leaves unanswered these questions: What *should* be the attrition rate in a school that advertises itself as a rehabilitative institution whose purpose is to retrieve marginal students? And what were such students led to believe about their chances of success when they were recruited by the college in the first place?

Retention is the corollary of attrition, and the college was vulnerable, as I discussed earlier, on its retention practices. It is one thing to maintain an open-door college and a second-chance college, for which good arguments can be made, but another to retain students on campus who repeatedly demonstrate their inability or disinclination to do the work. When the second chance becomes a third, fourth, or fifth chance, or when probationary students are allowed to remain indefinitely and in large numbers on the campus regardless of their performance, the college is unavoidably damaged. The academic program, the tone of student life, the general standards of the college are all bound to suffer. Not the least of the negative effects at Parsons was in worsening the already grave problem of student attitudes. Joseph Hichar, formerly a professor of biology at Parsons who left the college in 1965 to help organize one of the satellite colleges, recalls that, "When it developed that nobody at Parsons could get thrown out for academic reasons, and no one could get thrown out for disciplinary reasons, then the student body got fairly difficult to deal with. They got very cocky because they knew nothing would happen to them."

For most of Roberts's administration the college really had no retention policy. Or rather the retention policy was to retain everybody it was possible to retain. There is virtual unanimity on this point among past and present administrators at Parsons. Everett Hadley, vice president for student services at Parsons, comments:

Basically in the past, the way the retention business operated was that if a kid could afford to go here and wanted to go, within tolerable limits such as showing some modicum of progress—such as a grade point average of .74 to 1.0 [that is, "D–" or "D"]—the quaint old custom was that he could stick around. We had people who were here for two or three straight years and never hit a 2.0 [a "C" average].

A former leading administrator at Parsons in 1964–1965 put the whole matter this way to me:

When I was there, Parsons had no standards for admission and none for retention. In the catalogue we said that students would be dismissed after three semesters if they did not reach a certain grade average, but when we tried to dismiss them they were simply taken back in again. I sat on the admissions committee and it was almost a joke to see people who wanted to exclude certain students but didn't dare open their mouths.

For years there was no admissions committee. It was after the college had been put on probation by the North Central Association that we got a committee. And it was made up of some very conscientious professors who tried to do some screening, but that committee was not successful. For instance, when the committee was cleaning out some people at the bottom of the heap that we knew just couldn't succeed with all the tutoring in the world, then the idea came out of the promotional office that we might establish a special category for them. They were not to be real students, they were really nonstudents . . . they paid their full tuition and they sat in the classes—most of them did not go to class anyway—they were nondegree students. They were students who were really not college material but were students who were allowed to remain, and the idea was that if they were placed in this new category, North Central would not raise hell.

The negative effects on other students and on the college in general are not the only price that has to be paid for the lack of a retention policy, though that is a high price in itself. There is a serious question about the effects on the student himself who is retained when he ought to be dismissed. There is also a question about the motives of the institution. Is a college fulfilling its obligations to all its students when it allows and indeed encourages students who have demonstrated that they cannot succeed in the institution to remain and continue to pay fees? It may be a difficult line to draw, but a good many Parsons people saw it clearly enough. Keith Goltry, a long-time Parsons professor of education, said to me candidly: "I am guilty too and must share the responsibility. I knew what was going on but did not do anything." A former Parsons administrator, now at Albert Lea College, comments: "There were many cases of students who hung around for 12 or 15 trimesters and still could not graduate. There was one that had something like 37 trimesters! He was a fixture in the town. I flunked him in two courses myself, but he just kept coming back."

Whatever name one wants to apply to the Parsons retention practices, one cannot avoid the conclusion that the college, by going to such lengths to keep students on campus regardless of their academic performance and of the ensuing effects on the intellectual climate of the institution, deserved to be censured.

How Good Was the Teaching at Parsons?

As I outlined earlier, the teaching at Parsons was handled in the lower division by three classes of people from 1963 on. The ranked faculty did the principal lecturing; the preceptors were supposed to teach discussion groups of two or three dozen students; and the tutors taught students individually. The college had very mixed success with the preceptors and the tutors. About the only firm conclusion one can offer in regard to both groups is probably an obvious one: they were successful with most of the students, regardless of the level of ability, who went to them willingly and with a real desire to learn. The big problem was that so many students went grudgingly, although not actually compelled, and many more did not go at all.

The lecturing was somewhat different. The ranked faculty carried a teaching load of 12 to 15 hours, which meant four or five courses that met three times a week. That is a heavier load than is found at the better institutions now but about the same as at many lesser known institutions. Not many years ago it would have been regarded as a normal load at most institutions of higher education. At Parsons, however, the load was made heavier by the size of the classes, by the fact that every class was wholly given over to a fairly formal lecture, and by the emphasis that was put on good teaching. The Parsons professor worked hard by any comparative standard. "At Parsons," as one man said to me, "you do two men's work and get two men's pay."

How well the Parsons professor taught depended not only on his knowledge and talents but on how fully he was willing to devote himself to the special problems of lecturing at Parsons. I mean such special problems as how to lecture in the lower division to a class of 200 students with exceedingly diverse abilities and backgrounds. It is the same problem that high schools and junior colleges have, only in more aggravated form, in that the classes at Parsons were kept large for economic reasons and students were not divided into separate "tracks" or ability groups. How does one lecture on, say, classical Greece or French grammar to a class that spans the ability range from well above average to well below? And how does one pace a lecture or decide what intellectual plane to put it on when there is no interaction between lecturer and such heterogeneous groups of students?

Then there was for the Parsons lecturer the problem of how to deliver himself of three scintillating lectures a week to large classes when the subject matter demanded a different approach. Not all subjects lend themselves equally well to mass lecturing, but for financial reasons all subjects were treated as equal at Parsons. Thus professors of rhetoric, found themselves having to give several entire lectures on, say, the padding of themes by students—because that is what the syllabus called for. Teachers of foreign languages found themselves at a loss to know what if any part of the class had grasped either the grammar or the accent. Mathematics professors often had no way of knowing whether their students were moving through the lecture with them or not.

A lecturer is tempted to deal with these problems by disseminating information at the expense of insight or penetration. Cram teaching and cram learning is not easy to avoid in a situation as rigid as that at Parsons. The accumulation of knowledge tends to outweigh inquiry and understanding on the part of the student, a problem that was hardly limited to Parsons. In his analysis of Parsons, Ralph Cooper Hutchison found in 1959–1960 that,

> Some students who do pay some attention to the lectures brag that they can pass without "cracking" a book, even a textbook, because the lectures and recitations are only a re-hash of the text. Some courses under certain professors are exceptions, but it is generally possible for a student to attain respectable grades with a minimum of reading and study, and with no independent "thinking."[6]

In this respect Parsons resembled a large state university more than it did a private liberal arts college.

The situation was not greatly improved later when Parsons began recruiting people at high salaries who *said* they were interested in teaching. It is an open question whether a "teaching" faculty of the kind Roberts talked about is really possible. It is also a question whether one can put together a large faculty of people with doctorates who are willing to devote themselves to students who may not respond to the usual methods of college teaching; who are willing to make the extraordinary effort needed to develop new pedagogical techniques; who are willing to forego the stimulation of graduate students; who are committed to rehabilitative education; and who have the patience of Job. I don't know whether it is possible to build such a faculty or not, but it is certain that Parsons did not achieve it.

Yet it is not a disgrace to have failed, under financial and other pressures, to achieve what has not been achieved by any other institution. The Parsons faculty, whatever its limitations, was a hard working lot that did indeed give more attention to the quality of lecturing than do most faculties. There were a number of incentives to encourage the faculty to lecture well. The lectures were large in the lower division, and were also attended by the preceptors and tutors who were to repeat and reinforce the lecture material. In addition, the lectures were the principal means by which professors could entice students into particular majors and upper-division courses. Moreover, there is a good deal of personal testimony from students and observers attesting to the high quality of lecturing at Parsons—not to mention the fact that a number of academics outside the college who had some firsthand knowledge of Parsons sent their own children there because they felt the quality of teaching was higher than at other colleges to which their children might have gained admission.

The tendency of the Parsons teaching staff (lecturers, preceptors, and tutors) to put a premium on information, on "covering the material," had its effect on the Parsons library, which accumulated a good many aids to this kind of study. Yet, though Parsons spent a lot of money on the library as the college expanded, it could not keep up with the standards set by the American Library Association. When institutions reach 5,000 students, as Parsons did in 1966, they are rarely undergraduate colleges any longer; they usually have a graduate program. And ALA standards were established with that kind of library in mind. Because of its explosive growth, Parsons had to resort to buying books in quantity from mass lists and understandably found it difficult to build a selective, high-quality undergraduate library in a short time. Even if it had done so, I am not at all sure that Parsons students would have made the most of it. Parsons students taken *en masse* were not the sort to use a library in the way Thomas Carlyle talked about on the occasion of his being installed as the rector of the University of Edinburgh in 1866:

It remains, however, practically a most important truth, which I alluded to above, that the main use of Universities in the present age is that, after you have done with all your classes, the next thing is a collection of books, a great library of good books, which you proceed to study and read. What the Universities can mainly do for you— what I have found the University did for me, is, That it taught me to read, in various languages, in various sciences; so that I could go into the books which treated of these things, and gradually penetrate into any department I want to make myself master of, as I found it suit me.

I must add in fairness that most students are not Carlyles and not many of them on any campus make that kind of use of the institutional library. At Parsons, perhaps because of the rigid curriculum and instructional program, and perhaps because many of the students may have been more comfortable with facts than with ideas, both the teaching and the learning, especially in the core curriculum (where most of the students were to be found), tended to be textbook-based with an emphasis on mastery of information. Those who would criticize Parsons for that kind of education must be prepared to give the same treatment to a great many other institutions. Let us say, then, that when all is taken into account, the quality of teaching at Parsons compared well with that of most American institutions of what is called the higher learning and would have to be considered better than that of a great many.

We might then ask about grading standards. Would a "C" at Parsons be equal to a "C" at other institutions? Or were grading standards lowered to accommodate students of lower ability? As is not unknown in other institutions, there were administrative pressures on the faculty, of varying intensity at varying times and with varying success, to dilute grading standards. Also, the standards themselves varied greatly according to professors and departments, with the "soft" subjects such as elementary education and physical education consistently recording higher grades than other departments. But this is a common phenomenon.

On the whole I doubt that grading standards at Parsons were below those of other unselective private colleges. However, Parsons did go to extraordinary lengths to allow students to make the "C" average that they needed in order to keep in good standing and to graduate. There was, for example, a system of "starring" a student's transcript of credit. The system in effect allowed the student to continue to take a given course as many times as necessary to make at least a "C" in it. When he got his "C" or better, this grade supplanted, though it did not expunge, "D's" and "F's" or other grades that were on his record from previous attempts at the course. The new grade then became the only one used in the computation of his grade point average. Thus with stamina and the necessary funds a student could count on a more or less unlimited number of tries at his courses. It is commonplace in American colleges to allow a student to repeat a course in which he has an unsatisfactory grade, but less common to use only the higher grade in the computation of the grade point average.

There was also a system of "double starring" at Parsons. This system allowed a student to petition the college to strike out any elective course he might have flunked from his grade point average and from his accumulation of credits toward the degree. The course was kept on his record but double starred and was, in Parsons's terminology, "not accepted for graduation." Students could thus collect a number of low or failing grades in elective courses without prejudicing their grade point average or their degree as long as they took a sufficient number of additional courses to meet graduation requirements. One effect of this practice was, of course, to keep enrollments up. It was not a practice peculiar to Parsons, but it was certainly unusual.

In spite of these and other dubious devices used at Parsons for retaining students on campus, the "C" average needed for good standing and graduation had to be earned. The student had to sweat it out, however long it took. To help him, he had well-qualified professors who exposed him to a quality of lecturing that would compare favorably with that of a great many American institutions.

What Standardized Tests Show about Parsons Graduates

Another measure of an institution's quality is the performance of its seniors and graduates on certain standardized tests. This measure ignores, of course, the whole problem of attrition. It ignores all the students who drop out of an institution before graduation, or flunk out or transfer to another college. It is concerned only with students who actually take a degree. For a number of years, the Educational Testing Service at Princeton has offered a series of tests called the Graduate Record Examination to institutions of higher education. It is offered on two levels. The upper level of the GRE is required by most of the better graduate schools of the country, which use an applicant's scores on these exams as a major criterion for admission. The upper level was not used at Parsons and is not used by most undergraduate colleges. We therefore have no statistical way of measuring those graduates of Parsons who actually went on to graduate school against other graduate students.

The lower level of the GRE has nothing to do with admission to graduate school. From 1944 to 1968 it was known as the Institutional Testing Program and is now called the Undergraduate Record Examination. For our purposes here,

I will call it simply the URE. It is designed only for internal use by undergraduate colleges as a means of measuring their students against national undergraduate averages. Hundreds of colleges use the URE every year for their own purposes, chiefly as a means of self-assessment. In the 1968–1969 academic year, it was taken by about 170,000 students. Parsons used it for a number of years and continues to do so today, so that data from these tests afford one means of comparing Parsons students to those of other colleges.

The URE is composed of three standardized, multiple-choice, machine-scored tests. One is the "Aptitude Test" designed to measure the verbal and mathematical ability of college seniors. This test was not used at Parsons. One is the "Area Tests" designed to measure the student's achievement in three broad areas of knowledge—social science, humanities, and natural science. And one is the "Advanced Tests" designed to measure the student's achievement in his major subject of study and is available in twenty-two fields. Parsons used the Area Tests and the Advanced Tests. For a while it gave both tests three times each year—to its freshmen, sophomores, and seniors, thereby giving the college information about how much progress students made while in the institution. Parsons now gives the tests twice—to students at the time they enter the college, whether as freshmen or transfers, and to its seniors toward the end of their last semester.

One way of looking at the quality of a Parsons education is to ask how much increase there was in URE scores between the freshman and senior years or between the sophomore and senior years, and how these increases compare to national averages. This is a hazardous measure in view of the varying attrition rates at American colleges and a number of other uncertain conditions, but the Table 5–1 yields at least a suggestive comparison.

Or we can ask how the average scores of Parsons students

TABLE 5-1

Parsons Students' Increase in URE Area Tests Scores Compared to National Averages

	SOCIAL SCIENCE	HUMANITIES	NATURAL SCIENCE
Average increase in scores of *Parsons students* between freshman and senior years (1966 graduating class only)	63	17	18
Average increase *national group* between freshman and senior years	66	48	33
Average increase in scores of *Parsons students* between sophomore and senior years (for the period, 1962–1966)	48	25	19
Average increase *national group* between sophomore and senior years	43	30	23

(not the *rate* of increase) compare with national averages. The national averages or "norms" are not a yearly calculation but are fixed by ETS at one point in time by using a representative national sample of students and institutions. On this measure, we get Table 5-2.

TABLE 5-2

Parsons Students' Average Scores in URE Area Tests Compared to National Averages

	SOCIAL SCIENCE	HUMANITIES	NATURAL SCIENCE
Average score for *Parsons seniors*, 1961–1966	448	415	446
Average score for *Parsons seniors*, 1962–1967	460	427	458
Average score *national group*	489	494	487

We cannot do complete justice to the two tables above. In order to do so, we would have to decide, first, how good the

Area Tests themselves are (a complex question that I do not propose to tackle here); second, how the national averages were arrived at, what the participating schools were, what their attrition rates were, how they compared to Parsons in various ways, and so on; and third, how one would *expect* students who persisted to graduation at Parsons to compare with the graduates of other institutions.

In short, it's complicated; and we had better settle for an admittedly incomplete judgment. Social science at Parsons is the strongest of the three areas and Parsons students seem to progress in this area at rates comparable to those of students in other colleges. Parsons students show less progress in humanities and natural science, especially between their freshman and senior years. Apart from the rate of progress while in the institution, Parsons graduates consistently perform below, often well below, the graduates of other colleges—that is the graduates of the twenty-one institutions that were used by ETS in arriving at national averages (a potpourri of institutions like the State University of Iowa, Allegheny College, the University of Miami, and Whitman College).

Let's turn to the URE Advanced Tests, those concerned only with the student's major field of study. For a number of years, seniors at Parsons took these tests in eighteen subjects. Suppose we look at the results over two sets of years, 1961–1966 and 1963–1967. We should also look at these results in relation to the numbers of students involved, for the numbers in some subjects are too small to support any firm conclusion and so large in others as to lead to unwarranted conclusions if the numbers are not known. First, therefore, we should note that Parsons regularly turned out very large numbers of graduates in the fields of business and education, followed by economics and history. These four subjects made up over half of all Parsons graduates—63 per cent in the 1961–1966 period and 55 per cent in the 1963–1967 period. Table 5–3 shows the results for these four subjects.

TABLE 5–3

*Parsons Students' Average Scores in URE Advanced Tests
Compared to National Averages*

	NUMBER OF STUDENTS TAKING THE TESTS		AVERAGE SCORE OF PARSONS STUDENTS		AVERAGE SCORE OF NATIONAL GROUP
	1961–1966	1963–1967	1961–1966	1963–1967	
Education	444	408	384	401	409
Business	430	708	406	408	509
Economics	252	238	438	451	494
History	219	236	455	470	506
	1,345	1,590			

Thus in the subjects of greatest enrollment at Parsons, only in education do its graduates compare well to the national group, a fact that is made even less complimentary to Parsons when one remembers the generally low esteem in which education as a subject of study is held in American colleges and universities. Business as a subject of undergraduate study is not greatly higher in academic reputation than education. It turned out more graduates at Parsons than any other department, but scores for such students were more than one hundred points below the national average. Table 5–4 shows the scores in the other subjects in which the tests were taken at Parsons.

The national averages for all these tests are not as reliable as they might be. The sample of students and institutions on which they were based by ETS varied greatly in number in any given subject, as did the percentage of eligible students who actually took the tests within the institutions. Thus the national figures are a usable guide but a somewhat rough one. Taking the eighteen subjects together, Parsons graduates scored close to or above the national average on two of them, biology and chemistry. They scored somewhat below the national average on six other subjects. And they scored over

TABLE 5–4

*Parsons Students' Average Scores in URE Advanced Tests
Compared to National Averages*

	NUMBER OF STUDENTS TAKING THE TESTS		AVERAGE SCORE OF PARSONS STUDENTS		AVERAGE SCORE OF NATIONAL GROUP
	1961–1966	1963–1967	1961–1966	1963–1967	
Literature	145	64	443	439	548
Biology	106	137	482	497	495
Sociology	104	164	434	447	474
Psychology	101	141	341	425	512
Physical Ed.	90	114	347	342	439
Mathematics	77	67	447	503	542
Government	70	96	441	445	496
Chemistry	46	36	520	543	530
Music	20	12	366	386	481
Philosophy	18	16	442	466	549
Speech	15	10	413	359	474
Spanish	10	9	413	427	520
French	9	21	410	420	533
Physics	4	8	530	498	546
	815	1,263			

fifty points below the national average on the remaining ten subjects.

The comparisons I have been making in the above pages pit Parsons against a representive sample of all American institutions of higher education, a comparison that Parsons might claim, with some justice, is not appropriate for its own student body. (Unfortunately, the misleading claims to excellence that were made by the college's spokesmen from time to time invite just this kind of comparison, but still it is not a very fair comparison to make and leave standing without comment.) To get a more equitable comparison, suppose we look at the performance of Parsons graduates relative to that of the graduates of ten other colleges that Parsons thinks of as having comparable admissions policies. Although these institutions do not have nearly as high a proportion of transfer students as Parsons, they do follow a more or less open-door admissions policy. Parsons asked ETS to compare the Parsons scores in ten subjects of the Advanced Tests with those of ten other institutions that Parsons identified. Table 5–5 ranks the subjects according to the number of Parsons students involved (education being highest), and adds the national average as well as that for the ten colleges.

TABLE 5–5

Parsons Students' Average Scores in URE Advanced Tests Compared to Ten Comparable Colleges

	AVERAGE SCORE OF PARSONS SENIORS 1962–1967	AVERAGE SCORE OF STUDENTS AT 10 OTHER UNSELECTIVE COLLEGES	AVERAGE SCORE OF NATIONAL GROUP
Education	401	413	409
Economics	451	482	494
History	470	467	506
Sociology	447	447	474
Literature	439	491	548
Psychology	425	444	512
Biology	497	492	495
Government	445	445	496
Mathematics	503	449	542
Chemistry	543	488	530

The 10-college group used for comparison included such institutions as Arkansas State College, Furman University, Geneva College, and Hartwick University. Parsons comes off better in this kind of comparison than in a national competition. It holds its own with this group of ten unselective institutions, matching their graduates in two of the tests, outscoring them somewhat in four, and scoring below them in the remaining four.

What one makes of such statistical comparisons depends, as I have said, on what one makes of the URE. If one thinks of such standardized, machine-scored tests as suspect under the best circumstances, one might be inclined to minimize them in any assessment of Parsons or any other college. If one regards them as a generally reliable and a reasonable guide to the quality of education offered by an institution, one can look on them as saying a good deal about Parsons. Taking it all together, I feel that these tests corroborate other kinds of evidence about the quality of a Parsons education and indicate that the college, while not doing nearly as well as its press agents said it was, was doing a creditable job given the limitations under which it operated. At least it was offering, judging by its graduates, an education as good as that of other unselective American institutions.

Other Factors Relating to Quality

Parsons often made claims about the high proportion of its graduates that went on to graduate schools—which is another common measure of institutional quality. Parsons's claims in this regard, like those of other colleges, were often inflated. Most institutions do not or cannot keep precise records about the fate of all their graduates, and they frequently indulge in little more than guesswork about the numbers that go on to graduate schools.

The fact is that Parsons, as of this writing, does not really know how many of its students go on to graduate study, how long they stay, or with what success. It reported one study in 1968 of a group of 652 of its students who graduated between 1962 and 1967 and who before graduation had indicated their intention of going to graduate school. This group represented 23 per cent of the total graduates of the college during these years. Of the 652 graduates involved, 279 (44 per cent) responded to a questionnaire sent by the college; 129 of them said they were full-time graduate students, and 59 said they were part-time or summer graduate students.[7] Only 6 or 7 per cent, that is, of the total number of graduates during this six-year period are therefore known, at least by their own testimony, to have done some kind of graduate work. The actual number may well be higher but one does not know. Many of the students who did respond had been education majors at Parsons and were therefore presumably doing graduate work in a school of education. Such work is normally required of classroom teachers for advancement, and their ranks consequently swell the graduate enrollments everywhere; but the admissions standards and the quality of work done in these programs are open to some doubt.

Other estimates by Parsons of the number going on to graduate work vary from 60 or 70 per cent to 30 per cent, the latter being a figure often cited by people at Parsons. I do not know what the real figure is and doubt that Parsons does. Until reliable information is available, one must simply suspend judgment about where Parsons stands on this criterion of quality.

Still another way of trying to get at the quality of an institution is student opinion. This is likewise a hazardous means but perhaps not more so than other means frequently used. I tend myself to put a fair amount of weight on student opinion when it can be had from a large number of individuals. At Parsons there was never any rating of courses or professors by the students, as is frequently the case on other campuses; but there was in 1966 a formal attempt by the college to allow students to characterize life and learning at the college. To do so, Parsons used a kind of inventory of attitudes developed by the Educational Testing Services and known as the College and University Environment Scales

(CUES). This inventory consists of 150 true-false statements about colleges, about their facilities, student regulations, professors, curricula, examinations, student life, and so on. ETS says that the test is

> a device for obtaining a description of the college from its students themselves, who presumably know what the environment is like because they live in it and are a part of it. What the students are aware of, and agree with some unanimity of impression to be generally true, defines the prevailing campus atmosphere as students perceive it.[8]

Parsons students were asked to respond twice to each of the 150 statements, once to indicate whether or not they felt the statement to be true of Parsons, and once to indicate whether they felt it *should* be true of Parsons. The college thus got a "real-ideal" comparison in which its students indicated what they thought life was really like at Parsons and what they would prefer it to be like. The test was given to a sample of 127 students who had been two trimesters or more at Parsons and who were, according to the college, "representative of upperclassmen."[9]

The CUES test is composed of five "scales" called *practicality, community, awareness, propriety,* and *scholarship,* and the 150 statements all relate to one or another of these qualities as seen by the student about his own campus. The national averages or norms for this test were computed by ETS from the responses of students at forty-eight colleges and universities.

Using these national averages for comparison, Parsons found that its students rated the college average on only one scale, *practicality,* and below average on the other four scales. The greatest discrepancy between the "real" and the "ideal" was on the *scholarship* scale—indicating that to Parsons students themselves, the academic atmosphere of the college was far below what they would have liked it to be. The next greatest gap was on the *awareness* scale—indicating that the students felt Parsons to be well below average in the opportunities it afforded students to develop both "self-awareness" (through creative and artistic means) and political and social awareness. The next greatest gap was in *community*, a quality that one would expect more often in a college, especially one in a small town, than in a large urban university; but the verdict of the Parsons students reinforces my own observations that such a sense of unity, common purpose, and group welfare was not strong at the college.

Put another way, the students liked the social life (not the same as *community*) at Parsons—the accent on parties, sports, and informal group activity. They liked the personal and professional help they got, the rather rigid examination system for which they could make specific preparation, and the quality of the faculty. They did not like the general sloppiness of their fellow students, their lack of courtesy, their lack of aesthetic interest, and their tendency to a certain destructiveness. In spite of giving the faculty a vote of confidence, however, they testified that they were not stretched by Parsons classwork and did not find most of the courses "an intellectual challenge." On the whole, the CUES results, which put Parsons in the lower third of the national group against which it was comparing itself, were not very encouraging so far as the "real" Parsons was concerned but could be regarded as quite encouraging so far as the "ideal" that Parsons students themselves opted for.

On the matter of student opinion, I should also record for the sake of balance that a number of students to whom I and my research assistant spoke in 1967 and 1968 defended Parsons vigorously. While some students did indeed corroborate the CUES results, others spoke highly of the education they had got at Parsons—for example: "I will stack up my Parsons degree against any in the country." Some spoke of work they had done elsewhere and how it compared to Parsons—for example: "I took a summer course last year at NYU and it was a real dud by comparison with Parsons courses." Some admitted the school's limitations—for example: "The academic life and atmosphere is void except for a group of about forty students."

Perhaps the virtues of Parsons, as seen by its stoutest defenders among the students, are summed up in this taped conversation with an editor of the school paper:

I came here in 1965 after flunking out of the University of Connecticut twice. Now I am on the dean's list at Parsons. I have found myself; and for people like me the system works. I think about one out of three find themselves here. Parsons's students are well rounded people, especially men, who are going to be important people. They are not intellectually all wrapped up. The professors are excellent—I know most of mine personally and can talk to them about anything. Parsons is a big improvement over big, impersonal, unmotivating universities. The faculty is dedicated and not so hung up on research. The loss of accreditation [see Chapter 7] was just politics—jealousy on the part of the North Central Association—they didn't like Dr. Bob's dynamic character. He was quite a man.

While this view puts the best light on Parsons that may be possible, it is not an uncommon one among those students for whom "the system works."

Another point that should be made in regard to the quality of a Parsons education is that the restricted curriculum did not permit students to pile up, and count toward graduation, a lot of mickey-mouse elective courses of the kind that can be found on almost any campus, often in abundance. To be sure, Parsons students did spend more time in lower division courses than is customary elsewhere; and the college did turn out a big proportion of its students in such relatively un-demanding subjects as business and education. But there was at least a broad foundation of general education under all Parsons students, and there was rarely the kind of dilution of both lower and upper division work that is found at many colleges.

The point is clearly seen by looking at some transcripts of credit for Parsons graduates. An analysis of transcripts for a sample of recent Parsons graduates reveals that the catalogue requirements of both the core curriculum and the major were carried out in practice (a fact not always true of colleges), and that little opportunity was available at Parsons for stu-dents to fill electives with trivial or exotic courses, since few such courses were offered.

The transcripts do reveal, as I indicated earlier, that Par-sons was exceedingly lenient in discounting courses from a student's record (though not in eliminating them from the record) in which he had done badly, and allowing him to retake them as often as necessary or to substitute others for them in order to meet degree and grade requirements. In at least half the transcripts examined, adjustments of this kind had been made, ranging from the discounting of a single three-hour course in the case of one student to the discounting of thirty semester hours for another. In some instances the student would not have had a grade point average high enough to graduate if his "F's" and "D's" had also been counted into his grade point average and thus added to his total courses. I don't necessarily condemn this practice though it is clearly open to abuse. Nor do I know how widespread it may be among other colleges. I merely record it with raised eyebrows, wondering whether it was in the interest of the student, allowing him to free himself from an unsatisfactory past, or of the college, allowing it to retain as many students as possible.

Here are a few examples of the undergraduate programs of recent Parsons graduates as revealed in their transcripts of credit. I offer them as typical profiles of *successful* students at Parsons:

Case 1—A transfer student who ranked 182 in his high school graduating class of 222. He entered Parsons after doing college work at two other institutions. He was on probation at his previous institution and had a grade point average of about "D minus." He graduated from Parsons in 1968 after spending a total of twelve semesters (six years as normally calculated) in college. His grade point average on graduation was 2.3 (roughly a "C plus") and his major was sociology. Parsons "forgave" or discounted from his transcript a total of twenty-four semester hours of courses that he had done badly in, courses that, if they had been counted in his grade point average, would have lowered it below the "C" necessary for graduation. Table 5–6 shows the courses he successfully completed in his undergraduate career.

Here then was a student who looked extremely unpromising when he entered Parsons. As a flunk-out from other institutions, he would probably have been inadmissible at practically all tax-supported institutions, all private institutions of repute, and would have been regarded as a very poor bet at almost any institution. Yet he persisted at Parsons and finished with a broad collection of respectable courses, and left with a degree that would probably compare with that of many an American college, public or private.

Case 2—A female student who entered Parsons as a freshman from the lower half of her high school graduating class. She had low College Board scores (351 in the SAT verbal test and 316 in math). She flunked and then repeated one core course at Parsons but graduated in nine trimesters with a major in sociology. Her final grade point average was 2.70 (about a "B minus"). Her lower-division work was very similar to Case 1 above, and her upper-division work was mostly in sociology and psychology with some political science, history, and drama. Again, here was a student who would not

TABLE 5–6

Lower Division

SUBJECT	NUMBER OF COURSES	SEMESTER HOURS
Art	1	3
Biology	4	14
Drama	1	3
English (Rhetoric)	2	6
Geology	1	3
German	2	6
History	3	9
Humanities	4	12
Mathematics	1	3
Physics	1	3
Political Science	1	3
Psychology	1	3
Sociology	1	3

Upper Division

Business	2	6
Education	1	3
History	2	6
Psychology	4	12
Sociology	8	24
Grand total	40	122

have been admissible to the majority of institutions and who was clearly a chancy case, but who made it through her college career with no trivial courses and with a decent grade point average.

Case 3—A male transfer student with fairly good College Board scores (540 in the SAT verbal exam and 632 in mathematics) from the middle of his high school graduating class. He arrived at Parsons from his previous institution with a number of "C's" on his record sprinkled with some "D's" and "F's". Parsons discounted thirteen semester hours of work from his record and graduated him two years later with a "C" average and a major in business. Two-thirds of his upper-division work was in business, the rest in drama, economics, English, and history. His case is representative of a lot of transfer students at Parsons with good high school records, who had originally been admitted to good colleges but who, for whatever reasons, left these colleges and succeeded at Parsons.

Case 4—A male freshman student with divergent College Board scores (254 in the SAT verbal exam and 529 in math) who had finished high school in the last fifth of his class. He had a "C plus" average from the two colleges he previously attended. He spent six trimesters at Parsons and interspersed them with three trimesters at two other institutions, failed no courses, took lower-division work in twenty subjects, and upper-division work in business and economics. He graduated from Parsons with a grade point average of 2.40 (a "C plus").

I could go on with illustrations of this kind demonstrating that the Parsons system did indeed work for many students. That it did *not* work for many others is clear from the attrition rate and other factors I have already discussed. Those who were successful at Parsons earned degrees that did not, as has been widely believed, debase the academic coinage. Parsons did have its gimmicks for keeping people on campus and paying their fees, and must be held accountable for them; it did allow many of its students to count more lower division courses toward the degree than other colleges might do; it did discount unsatisfactory courses from a student's record more liberally than most institutions probably do; its students did tend toward the less rigorous academic majors in the upper division; it did lack intellectual zest, a sense of unity and common purpose, and many other things.

But these deficiencies were not unique to Parsons. Indeed some of Parsons's shortcomings can be found on many a prestige campus, and perhaps all of its shortcomings can be found among some of our smaller and poorer colleges, public and private. Parsons did have a faculty that would compare favorably with the majority of undergraduate colleges and would outstrip a great many; it did provide more personal attention to its students than do most institutions; it did offer a tougher and more restricted curriculum than many colleges; and it did take in very large numbers of students with unpromising or dismal prospects and did manage to salvage many of them.

The problem in arriving at a true assessment of the quality of a Parsons education is not made easier by the claims that were made for the college by its press agents. Parsons never did as much or as well as its representatives claimed. So we must frankly conclude that for a very large number of students who left Parsons without a degree, a Parsons education was not a success, whatever they may have been led to believe in coming. Whether one prefers to regard this fact as evidence of the toughness of Parsons's standards or of their weakness depends on what one expects a college to do for a student body like that of Parsons. What is clear is that Parsons, like a great many other American institutions, offered an education that could not be successfully completed by a high proportion of the students it admitted.

Nevertheless, when one forgets the overblown claims and looks only at the students who did succeed, one must say that the college graduated a lot of students with creditable degrees for which no apology need be made. The quality of a Parsons education for these students will compare well with that of unselective colleges in general and possibly with that of some selective institutions as well.

NOTES

[1] Clarence J. Bakken, "High School Grades in Relation to College Success," mimeographed (1963).

[2] "Attrition at Parsons College, 1950–1965," Office of Institutional Research of Parsons (April 12, 1966).

[3] "Enrollment Trends during the Trimester Period, 1960–1965," Office of Institutional Research of Parsons (January 5, 1966).

[4] Robert J. Panos and Alexander W. Astin, "Attrition among College Students," *American Educational Research Journal* (January, 1968), pp. 57–72.

[5] Pearl Max, "How Many Graduate?" Office of the Coordinator of Institutional Research, City University (November, 1968).

[6] Ralph C. Hutchison, *A Study on the Utilization of Teaching Resources at Parsons College*, I, Chap. 3 (1960), 1.

[7] *Basic Institutional Data* (Parsons College, 1968), p. 60. Still another questionnaire was sent in 1968 to 2,500 Parsons graduates about graduate work. Data from this study are not available as of this writing.

[8] "College and University Environment Scales," ETS (1963), p. 2.

[9] "The Institutional Climate at Parsons College," Office of Institutional Research at Parsons (January 20, 1967), p. 1.

6: Parsons and Its Critics

Many of the people here were like myself. They would not stand up to the administration because when they came here, they came for the money and they figured that they would take the college for all they could while they were here. The college on the other hand figured it would take them for all it could. And as a result we had a continual problem.

—A PARSONS PROFESSOR

The trouble with Parsons is that there are always so many rumors, and what is worse, they are usually true.

—A PARSONS STUDENT

To do good is noble; to tell others to do good is also noble and a lot less trouble.

—MARK TWAIN

Although any sizable departure from orthodoxy in education is likely to draw critical fire, Parsons drew much more than was necessary and more than another college following the same radical ideas might have. As is no doubt clear by now, people tend to have strong opinions about Parsons. Their assessments range from the comment of one student, "It's Evilsville, man—the whole place is a pit of snakes," to this one by another student:

It was Parsons that gave me the opportunity to begin college on scholarships, grants and loans and afforded me a chance to maintain a full-load curriculum and still enable me to carry a work-load by employing me in the student commons and other areas. It is my full desire that Parsons and the friendly and extremely pleasant town of Fairfield get the recognition they both deserve.

And not a few other students share the feeling of one who said, "Parsons had plenty going for it until the Establishment got worried and busted Dr. Bob."

Because Parsons *was* Roberts in so many ways, one has no easy job in trying to separate opinion about Roberts from that about the college. There was always a wide middle ground of views that supported the Parsons Plan while criticizing the execution of it, but opinion did tend to polarize during Roberts's time on the campus, the preponderance of opinion at the negative pole. With the possible exception of the first year or two of his administration, Roberts always had more critics than advocates, more enemies than friends, and the ratio increased to the end.

The Parsons Credibility Gap

One of the earliest and most persistent criticisms of both Roberts and the college was that they, to put it charitably, lacked candor. Educators who followed the fortunes of the college began eventually to talk about "the Parsons credibility gap" and the gap got wider as the publicity got greater. Raymond Gibson, provost of the college under Roberts, wrote an article, which I have cited before, after he left Parsons called "The Scholarch of Parsons and the NCA" in which he commented that "The NCA [the North Central Association] accused Parsons and its president of a credibility gap; but the NCA was wrong. There was in fact a credibility canyon."[1] Even among educators who knew little about Parsons beyond what they had heard, there was a general uneasiness and lack of confidence. Almost from the beginning, the college was suspected of distorting information about itself and of misleading the public and the educational community. Together with the publicity, this was most responsible for bringing about the decline and fall of both Roberts and his college.

The credibility gap was fed not so much by outright lies as by evasions, half-truths, unsubstantiated claims, and by unorthodox methods of gathering and reporting data or a disinclination to do so at all. Roberts issued to members of the Parsons faculty and staff a handbook called "Manual for the Instructional Staff, 1964–1965." Under the subtitle, "Academic Freedom," the following directive is given: ". . . as an educational officer of the college, he [each professor or administrator] has the positive responsibility of being accurate [and of] exercising restraint whenever appropriate." If Parsons had minded this directive, the credibility gap might not have existed. Because the credibility gap is a central factor in the Parsons story, we need to look at a variety of examples, say ten, in order to be clear about just what it was and what forms it took. I do this at some length because an understanding of the credibility gap is indispensable to an understanding of the criticisms of Parsons that circulated widely in the academic world.

Example 1: As I indicated in Chapter 5, Roberts's irrepressible talk about the profit that Parsons was making probably did the most to arouse the suspicion and distrust of other educators. To counteract this suspicion, Roberts would sometimes promise his critics to clarify what he meant by the term *profit*, or he would promise to leave off using the word entirely. The Iowa College Foundation, for instance, a group of nonprofit colleges to which Parsons belonged, and its industrial contributors became so concerned in 1966 with Roberts's claims that they fought the issue out with him at their summer meeting that year and issued the following statement:

> Information provided by Dr. Roberts indicates that Parsons College is not a profit-making institution, does not claim to be and is about to undertake an extensive communicative effort to correct false impressions given by previous publicity. An audit is being made available to contributors and colleges.

At about the same time the board of review in Parsons's home county threatened to make Parsons pay property taxes in view of its claim that it was a profit-making institution.

Even when Roberts made clear what he meant by profit, journalists often got the amount wrong by, as the engineers say, several orders of magnitude. The June 26, 1966 issue of the St. Louis *Post-Dispatch*, for example, reported that Parsons had made a profit of $9 million in the 1965–1966 year —which was nearly three times the actual figure—while *Life* magazine at almost the same time said the amount was $8 million. As early in Roberts's administration as August, 1960, *Time* magazine in a laudatory piece on Parsons reported: "The debts are gone; the college is self-supporting from student fees alone." In fact the debts were by no means gone, as one of the Parsons trustees pointed out in a private letter to the magazine.

The claim that Parsons made a profit was not a lie, as we saw in Chapter 2. It was a typical sort of half-truth that seriously misled a great many people. It also made a major contribution to the Parsons "credibility gap."

Example 2: Roberts was careless with statistics about the college. In his speeches and reports and interviews with the press he liked to illustrate the spectacular progress that Parsons had made under his guidance. He would claim, for in-

stance, that the college had been offering no fewer than 768
courses when he took over, a staggering and even laughable
number in relation to the enrollment, and that he had
promptly chopped out 500 of them. In fact, the Parsons College *Bulletin* listed 341 possible courses for the 1954–1955
year, and the number actually scheduled was a good deal
lower than that.

Or he would say something like this: "In 1955, Parsons had
159 paid applications for admission that year. In 1966–1967,
it will have more than 14,000 paid applications . . ."[2] The
same astonishing number, 14,000, turns up in many other
places, especially in press reports quoting Roberts. The highest number of paid applications the college ever had in any
one year, according to Charles F. Barnett, head of the Parsons
admissions office, was slightly over 7,000. Roberts might say
that he was only being logical in this claim, that the college
two years earlier had received 3,500 paid applications, that
this number had doubled to 7,000 the next year, and that he
was only doubling it again as a logical projection. By the
same reasoning, of course, he could have claimed 28,000
paid applications for the year after that, leading to 56,000
the year after that, but that would have been comedy instead
of ambiguity.

In December 1967, six months after his departure from
Parsons, Roberts said to me: "At the end, we were getting
10,000 paid applications and taking 2,700 of them." In July,
1969 in another interview with me he went back to the figure
of 14,000 and claimed that by putting the "right" group of
three trimesters together one could get that figure. Later in
the same interview, he admitted that Parsons always took
everybody it could get. At any rate it was the inconsistent
claims of many kinds, unsupported by clear explanations, that
kept the credibility gap in good health and constantly growing during Roberts's administration. It was also the kind of
claim that prompted one Fairfield resident to say to me, re-

calling Roberts's regime: "I got tired of having to divide everything the college said by two."

Example 3: Roberts frequently made distorted claims about Parsons's graduates. In his speeches, he would say such things as:

> The 1962 graduating class at Parsons found 42 per cent of the seniors moving directly to graduate schools across America, and their records are excellent. Many of these students entered Parsons with minimal records behind them, but forced to meet high faculty and student standards, they were able to do work at an ever-increasing level of quality.[3]

Without worrying about what "high standards" or other phrases might mean in such a passage, suppose we look only at the statistics. The number of Parsons graduates who went on to graduate school in any given year is an exceedingly difficult and speculative calculation to make simply because reliable information on such matters was not gathered by Parsons. But there was no evidence to support the statement that 42 per cent of Parsons's graduates moved "directly to graduate schools," as Roberts claimed.

Typical of the earlier "research" done at Parsons on such questions was a study made in 1963. The college sent out 500 questionnaires to a "random sampling" of its graduates from 1955 through 1962; 140 questionnaires came back address unknown, leaving 360 that presumably were delivered to an address that might reach the intended recipient; 202 of these were actually filled out and returned; 70 of these— that is, 35 per cent of those who filled out the questionnaire —*claimed* that they were then doing some kind of full-time or part-time graduate work, or *claimed* that they had been in graduate school at some time in the past. From this informa- tion the college broadcasts to the world that 35 per cent of its graduates go on to graduate school.[4] One hopes that any Parsons student in an elementary statistics course who perpetrated such a report would be flunked.

Example 4: Roberts often made inaccurate or ambiguous claims about the Parsons program. On many occasions he claimed that the college was following a one-third–one-third–one-third admissions policy (see Chapter 3), but in fact such a policy was never followed. Or he would give a speech in which sweeping claims for the quality of education at Parsons were made. He would say, for instance:

> . . . Parsons has worked for years with varying levels of students, moving the poorly-prepared student into a remedial program, the average student at a normal pace, and the talented student at higher levels of challenge. This makes it possible for Parsons to accept students of varying academic backgrounds and to move them from where they are to a point as far as they can go.[5]

That is the sort of statement that makes experienced educators grind their teeth. They know how incredibly difficult it would be for any college, under the best circumstances, to do what Roberts said Parsons was doing. But that consideration aside, Parsons did not have anything that would be considered by most educators a sustained remedial program for most of Roberts's administration and never achieved anything as startling as this statement suggests.

Example 5: Misleading statements were frequently fed to the press and were duly printed therein for general consumption. Statements like the following often showed up in national publications: "Dr. Roberts denies that Parsons coddles its students. 'Of all low-achievers who enter, 76 per cent graduate,' he declares. 'Over-all, 87 per cent of our students earn a degree.'" The first figure turns on what a "low-achiever" at Parsons was, but as this term is understood in the rest of the world of higher education, the figure given could not be accurate or even close. The second figure is dead wrong: at no time during Roberts's administration did the college graduate 87 per cent of the students who entered. An expert in institutional research brought to Parsons by Roberts in 1965 comments: "I happen to know of one incident where a report had been submitted to Roberts which showed the actual attrition rate of freshmen students, and when he was asked this question at a public meeting a short time later, he gave an entirely different figure—a more complimentary one, of course."

Or a local newspaper would report Roberts as did this one after a speech of his in Council Bluffs, Iowa in January 1963: "One reason for Parsons's phenomenal rise, he said, was its average faculty salary of $18,500, one of the highest among private colleges in the nation." In the 1962–1963 year, the average faculty salary at Parsons was about $10,500.

Or take the professional journal, *College and University Business,* which published an admiring interview with Roberts in April, 1966 in the form of questions and answers. In it Roberts claimed that Parsons had "14,000 paid applications this year" and that it took only 2,400 of them. (See my earlier comments on the validity of this claim.) He referred to a study which he said demonstrated "that less than one student out of every six we've taken [at Parsons] in ten years transferred from anywhere else. We don't take any more flunk-outs than anybody else." The facts are that in the fall trimester of 1964, for example, Parsons admitted 600 freshmen and 393 transfer students; in the fall of 1965 it admitted 531 freshmen and 451 transfer students; in the fall of 1966 it admitted 487 freshmen and 652 transfer students. When I asked Roberts about his claim that Parsons did not take "any more flunk-outs than anybody else," he said that he really meant *somebody* else—that is, that one could find another college somewhere that took as many flunk-outs as Parsons.

In the same interview in *College and University Business*, Roberts said: "The tutors [at Parsons] earn from $9,000 to $12,000 and the preceptors approximately $11,000 to $15,000." In fact the range of salaries for tutors in 1966 was from $5,000 to $8,000, and the average salary for tutors was $6,279. The range for preceptors was $7,000 to $15,000, and the average salary was $10,272. On the Parsons budget, Roberts said: "Our total operating budget this year was $14.6 million. Our expenditure is $9 million, so we have excess income of $5.2 million." Parsons's budget for that year, according to its audit, was $13.2 million and its excess income about $3 million.

Example 6: Then there is the question of Roberts's degrees. For years Roberts listed himself in many places as the holder of two degrees from Yale University, an M.A. in 1941 and a Bachelor of Divinity in 1942. Or sometimes he listed only the bachelor's from Yale and shifted the master's to the University of Chicago. For instance, the biographical sketch of Roberts sent out by the Department of Ministerial Relations of the Presbyterian Church in 1955 at the time he was being considered for the presidency of Parsons lists him as having a Bachelor of Divinity from Yale in 1942 and an M.A. from the University of Chicago in 1943. A later *vita* headed "Biographical Information Concerning Dr. Millard G. Roberts" lists both the B.D. and M.A. degrees from Yale, as does the literature published by Consultants, Inc., one of Roberts's organizations. The succeeding issues of the Parsons *Bulletin*, up to the 1966–1967 number, lists him with an M.A. from Yale. The first edition of the 1966–1967 *Bulletin* makes a small change: it lists him with a master's degree but without identifying any awarding institution; the second edition of that year deletes the master's degree entirely. He is listed in *Who's Who in America* with an M.A. from Chicago, up to the

1968–1969 edition, which deletes any mention of a master's degree.

The fact is that Roberts did not hold a master's degree from either Yale or Chicago. He studied at Yale Divinity School from 1939 to 1941 but did not receive a B.D., an M.A., or any other degree while there. He does have a B.A. from Syracuse University in 1939, a B.D. from Chicago in 1942, and a Ph.D. from Chicago in 1947.

Example 7: If one checks the standard references on American colleges and universities—which, unfortunately, must rely on the institutions themselves for information—one finds the same tendency to distortion in the material on Parsons. In one major reference volume, Parsons claims to follow a "selective admissions policy to achieve a cross section of college-age population." In another Parsons is listed as having "an honors program open to all students." In another it is listed as accepting in 1963 and 1964 "about 50 per cent of applicants," of following a general admissions policy that it did not really follow, and of having arrangements whereby "students who have poor records on entering are placed in workshops where they receive intensive orientation courses to teach them proper study habits."

Another reference volume says of Parsons that "At the end of the freshman year, only 10 per cent of the students drop out and 75 per cent remain to graduate. Approximately 30 per cent of the graduates continue their education in graduate or professional schools . . . If the SAT is presented, scores must be above 450. . . . Of the 7,500 students who recently applied, 2,350 freshmen were enrolled."[6] Each of these statements is, to say the least, misleading.

Example 8: The institutional propaganda indulged in by Parsons had a cumulative effect which was enough to give pause even to people predisposed in favor of Roberts and the college. While most institutions naturally put their best foot forward in their official publications, Parsons often wound up with its foot in its mouth by carrying its boasting to self-defeating lengths. Illustrations can be found throughout Parsons's literature. Here are a couple:

> To achieve the goals of the unique program at Parsons, the college has acquired a qualified faculty second to none. Not only do they represent brilliant intellectual resources themselves, they also possess the intense desire and belief in the philosophy of working directly with the student. Careful screening has brought these individuals to Parsons, and their intellectual records are a result of years of teaching and specialized study.[7]

What makes such a passage distasteful is not that it lies (let's not quibble over whether such a phrase as "a qualified faculty second to none" is untrue or only poetic license) but that it lacks decent restraint. Such institutional swaggering offends but does not deceive other educators. It becomes serious when one remembers that the publication involved was used (and was still being used in the fall of 1968) to attract parents and students, who have no way of assessing such extravagant and self-serving claims.

Or consider statements of the following sort, which were sprinkled through a Parsons research report that was prepared to still some of the criticism of the standards of the college:

> To remove any question concerning the ability of the graduates who have received their education at Parsons, the college undertook one of the most comprehensive, longitudinal [sic] studies ever conducted on its graduates by an educational institution. . . .

> Such statistical facts as these should disquiet [sic] any doubt as to the creditability of grades received at Parsons College, since there can be no question that the Parsons

graduates have achieved outstanding academic records in graduate schools. . . .

For a college to literally open its books and reveal to the general public such detailed, statistical data on its graduates, as has been approved for release in this article, is unheard of and another revolutionary step in educational circles.[8]

Such naive, defensive, hortatory declamations, even if true (and they were not wholly true), would embarrass any self-respecting institution. Other educators reading such statements are bound to hold the sponsoring institution in contempt.

Lest I be thought to be singling out isolated statements by individuals, suppose we look at the Parsons College *Bulletin,* the institution's principal public document. Let us take a year in the middle of Roberts's reign, say 1963. The *Bulletin* for that year opens with this paragraph:

During the past six years, Parsons College has received national recognition as the fastest-growing college in Mid-America. One of the first two schools of higher learning to institute the Trimester System, it has also developed a curriculum which is being studied by many colleges and universities. By combining the lecture method with discussion sections, Parsons has moved to nearly double the contact hours in its courses. The Workshop System, through which Parsons has had outstanding success with the "average" student in difficult college courses, is known across America.

What is wrong with this, again, is not that it contains outright lies but that it distorts the truth. Laymen reading it would be unlikely to know, for instance, that the workshop system was not known "across America" at all and was anything but an "outstanding success" (it was converted a short time later to another system). Few educators would be misled, but parents and prospective students might easily conclude from such a passage that Parsons enjoyed a reputation in the world of higher education quite unlike the one it had in 1963.

Too much of the *Bulletin* was written in this inflated idiom. The leitmotif recurred often, as in this passage:

> Today Parsons ranks in the upper 10 per cent of all American colleges, with 71 per cent of its full-time faculty holding the earned doctorate. . . . Parsons College stands among the first colleges in the Middle West in recognition of its scholastic merit. Since the formation of national agencies of accreditation, Parsons has ranked with the leading colleges and universities of the nation. . . . Parsons is known for its remarkable success with the "average" student.

Anyone who was aware of Parsons's general reputation in American education in 1963 could not help but gag at seeing the college blatantly claim in its principal public document that it stood "among the first colleges of the Middle West in recognition of its scholastic merit," or that it was "known for its remarkable success with the 'average' student."

Most American institutions below the top rank are probably guilty in one way or another of overstating their virtues, and certainly of understating their limitations. Or of lapsing into a theatrical sales pitch—as in the case, for example, of a college in New York City that likes to advertise itself as "A beacon of innovation illuminating the concrete forest of the night." But Parsons had the habit of carrying to extremes abuses that might be common enough among other institutions. The motto on the Parsons College seal is *Est Modus in Rebus* ("There is a mean in all things"). If the promoters of

Parsons had kept it in mind, a far different history might have been written from 1955 to 1967.

Example 9: The experiences of individual visitors to Parsons added substantially to the credibility gap over the years. Most visitors "saw what Roberts wanted them to see," as Paul Vonk, academic vice-president of Parsons from 1963 to 1965, observes. Many laymen went away convinced that Roberts was a genius and Parsons a panacea. Knowledgeable educators, however, were taken in by package tours less often. Most of them who visited the campus and later wrote or talked about the institution complained of the difficulty of tracking down reliable information. One experienced consultant, for instance, who spent several days at the college in 1965 and several more in 1966 recalls being told that the Parsons trustees had set an astonishing goal of 15,000 students for the college. When he expressed his dismay, Roberts assured him that the trustees had had second thoughts and had decided against any more growth for a while. The visitor then said to me: "I went from there to the Director of Admissions, who told me, 'You're damned right we are not going to grow for a while—we can't get the students.' This kind of double talk was characteristic at Parsons."

Example 10: Perhaps the most appropriate way for me to end this melancholy part of the Parsons story is to record my own experience with the credibility gap. I think I have done more work on Parsons than any other "outsider," talked to more people, read more documents, gathered more data. One of my most frustrating problems throughout has been the difficulty of getting facts pinned down. I regret to say that in the course of this study I have encountered more lies and attempts at deception on the part of more people than I would have thought possible when I began.

To take just one illustration of many: early in my study I had heard in various places about the college's rather elaborate recruiting system (which I discussed in Chapter 3) with its payment by the head for recruiters and for people on campus who advised students. This is an unusual practice considered unethical by professional organizations, and I wanted to determine the real facts. But because the subject is, to say the least, a delicate one that many people would like to forget, getting the facts was almost impossible. I was told lies by a number of people who knew the truth.

I encountered similar behavior from some people in regard to a number of other subjects. Sometimes simple lies, more often subtle evasions and deceptions. Although I would of course have preferred silence to lies, the fact that I was lied to is not important. Nobody was under any obligation to tell me anything. Few people, however, seemed to take advantage of the fact and to decline to discuss Parsons with me; most people were willing to talk, if reluctantly, anonymously, and often in confidence—usually with the office door closed. I am only adding a bit of personal testimony to that of many other people to indicate that the Parsons credibility gap was real and was a big problem.

Perhaps none of these examples taken singly suggests the importance of the problem. But take them together, add the individual experiences of many persons whose opinions got around the academic world, add many other instances that I have not tried to review here of public misinformation in college documents and in the press, add rumors by the hundreds —and one can see how the college's credibility gap developed and how it provided the critics of Parsons College with plenty of ammunition. (I hasten to point out to the reader that I have discussed the credibility gap in the past tense. The college is now conducting its affairs, as I will discuss in the Epilogue, quite differently from the way it did in Roberts's administration. It is now much more restrained and accurate in its public statements and is now gathering extensive and reliable data on its own operations. While the college will unavoidably suffer for some time in the future from the credibility gap of 1955–1967, it now has far better and more complete information about itself than a very large number of American colleges and universities.)

The View from the Campus

Some of Roberts's most severe critics were in his own backyard, though people employed by the college were more often subdued than noisy in their criticism. The record of the Parsons faculty in opposing Roberts is, to say the least, spotty. As a corporate body it rarely resisted the administration, but individual faculty members and small groups were less intimidated. Life at Parsons seemed to produce little groups of boat-rockers who got themselves labeled by Roberts's supporters as, for example, "The Dissident Six," "The Seven Dwarfs," or "The Disgruntled Eight" (there was also a "Filthy Five" but they were supporters rather than opponents of the administration). These groups had innumerable complaints that all came back to one grievance, which most members of the Parsons faculty, openly or secretly, shared: one-man rule.

Roberts of course did not invent authoritarian administration. Many an American college president whose fiefdom has been a small church-related college or a public teachers college has spent a professional lifetime as a benevolent despot. But Roberts's brand of governance was often less than benevolent or discreet. He also made the mistake of hiring a lot of Ph.D.'s who had been trained up in a different tradition, who did not take the one-big-happy-family-under-daddy view of their role at Parsons, and who thought the faculty should have a major voice in running the college. He made the further mistake of thinking that the deliberate fostering of instability and conflict within the faculty would prevent organized opposition to the administration. To the extent that such organized opposition was prevented, it was due more to the reluctance of highly paid professors to jeopardize their jobs than to what might be called Roberts's Rules of Disorder.

Nor were Parsons's other administrators much admired. The faculty generally seemed to feel that anemic academic leadership was supplied by the panoply of deans and vice presidents that Roberts appointed and changed with great frequency. They had titles but no more power than Roberts was willing to yield them at any given point. Even if he relinquished some, he could quickly reclaim it. One leading Parsons professor, writing in 1966 to some of his colleagues, remarked that "only one administrator has remained in his position of authority for any length of time in the writer's three years at Parsons. He is, of course, President Roberts. Beneath him an inordinant [sic] number of men posed for varying lengths of time as Dean of one thing or another." Harold Eastman, head of the Parsons sociology department and more sympathetic than others with the problems of administrators trying to work under Roberts, comments that "they were good people but never had any authority to act. That is the story of Parsons College."

Roberts was criticized by the faculty for other things besides unilateral government. Off and on, faculty members criticized his refusal to support their departments adequately while he squandered funds on unessential matters and simultaneously boasted in public of the amount of money the college was making. They criticized what they thought of as capricious and discriminatory salary policies. They criticized him for nepotism in keeping his wife on the payroll as a full professor (and allowing an artificial lake on the campus to be named after her), though they recognized her as an outstanding teacher. They criticized him for his policies on grades, on admission and retention of students, and on standards in general. They criticized him for not knowing much about education and for not being willing to learn. And for many other things. But most of the complaints came back to the central issue of depriving the faculty of policy-making power.

One cannot help speculating on what really would have been different at Parsons if the faculty had actually been given the kind of authority it enjoys on other campuses. Some changes would certainly have been made, but perhaps not as many as one would expect. Faculty members are often more willing to demand power than to invest the time necessary to exercise it well. They complain bitterly about the number of committees they serve on and the length of deliberations, but respond even more bitterly if the administration threatens to relieve them of these onerous duties. A recent study of the American Council on Education comments on this common situation:

> One of the most noticeable and best documented findings of the investigation is the existence of a pervasive ambivalence in faculty toward participation in decision making. The faculty members interviewed overwhelmingly indicated the faculty should have a strong, active, and influential role in decisions, especially in those areas directly related to the educational function of the university. At the same time, the respondents revealed a strong reticence to give the time such a role would require. Asserting that faculty participation is essential, they placed participation at the bottom of their professional priority list and deprecated their colleagues who do participate. Reluctant to assume the burden of guiding institutional affairs, they seemed unwilling to accord others the responsibility for doing so. And while quick to assert their right to participate, they recognized less quickly the duties participation entails.[9]

At Parsons some reforms would certainly have been made if the faculty had demanded and been granted genuine, as distinct from showcase, power. How many reforms would have been effected and with what results can only be conjecture, of course. There was only one notable occasion on which a group of faculty members moved as a unit against Roberts. They produced a report which ultimately became famous.

The Dissident Report

In March, 1963 a document prepared by six distraught professors at Parsons, five of them younger members of the faculty and all of them relatively new at the college, became the first serious, organized opposition to Roberts from within the kingdom. It was a forty-two-page report titled *Conditions at Parsons College under the Administration of President Millard G. Roberts* and was accompanied by several dozen exhibits. It came to be called The Dissident Report or sometimes The Black Report. It contained a series of charges chiefly against Roberts but included some of the other Parsons administrators at certain points.

The Dissident Report was prefaced with a statement by the six authors, explaining that they were interested only in bringing what seemed to them scandalous conditions to the attention of the proper authorities. They alluded to former colleagues who had left the college out of disillusionment and other colleagues who had been lured to Parsons only to be deceived or abused. They accused the Parsons administration of fraudulent advertising and exploitation of students and parents. And they expressed the hope, not that their judgments would be taken at face value, but that their testimony on conditions at Parsons would be taken as grounds for a full-scale investigation by outside authorities to determine the true situation. The body of The Dissident Report then went on to charge (1) that the Parsons administration in its search for students was misleading the public with false or exaggerated claims; and (2) that Parsons was failing as an educational institution.

In support of these charges, the authors cited a good many discrepancies between claims and actuality in Parsons's publications. They discussed a variety of abuses relating to course offerings, salaries, faculty degrees (prematurely listed in the catalogue), the percentage of doctorate holders on the faculty, how much teaching Roberts himself did or failed to do, and the workshop and "associate" system (forerunner of the team teaching system). The report compared courses given with those advertised in the catalogue, compared the advertised admissions policy with the actual one, did the same with the average class size, with attendance policies, with the availability of tutoring and of professional counseling, and with dormitory overcrowding. The report discussed grading problems in some detail, alleging pressures from the administration to control the number of low grades, to change some grades already given, and otherwise to manipulate the grading process at the college for financial reasons.

Finally, the authors turned to the moral and intellectual climate of the college, alleging that the atmosphere of the college was heavy with suspicion, fear, and guilt that affected both students and faculty members. They condemned the practice of retaining students indefinitely who could not or would not do the necessary work. And they discussed violations of faculty contracts, misleading lures thrown out by the administration to tempt professors to come to Parsons, and charged Roberts with incredible personal abuse of some professors who opposed him in one way or another.

Many of the specific allegations and incidents discussed in the report, some of which I have mentioned above, were true; some, which I have not mentioned, were untrue. And some were petty whether true or not. But the principal broad charges were true and were similar to the conclusions arrived at later by a visiting team from the North Central Association. In putting their indictment together, the six authors had been discreetly helped by a considerable number, perhaps twenty, of the other faculty members as well as by some outsiders, including the local Presbyterian minister in whose church the first edition of The Dissident Report had been mimeographed.

The dissidents first sent their report to the chairman of the Parsons board of trustees and to the Board of Visitors (a church body that visited and evaluated the college each year). They also sent it to the American Association of University Professors in the expectation that the AAUP, with its active concern for the protection of academic freedom and tenure, would want to send an observer to Parsons when an investigation by the trustees or the church was made. Much to their chagrin, however, the AAUP declined to jump in but instead decided to wait to see if other official bodies would take any action. "Here was the worst scandal in American education in our century," says a leader of the dissident group, "and the AAUP would not go in." The AAUP did stay abreast of the Parsons situation and did visit the college in 1965. It did not find, according to Bertram Davis, general secretary of the AAUP, "a serious violation of academic freedom and tenure," but did recommend greater faculty involvement in governing the college.

Nor did satisfactory action seem to be forthcoming from the trustees or the church. The dissidents therefore sent their report to the rest of the Parsons trustees and to the regional accrediting association (the North Central Association of Colleges and Secondary Schools), where it precipitated an NCA visit to the college that in turn resulted in Parsons being placed on "public probation" for two years (see Chapter 7).

On the campus, it precipitated the appointment of a twelve-man committee, composed mostly of deans and other administrators, to rebut the report. It also precipitated, as I have mentioned, an investigation of the six dissidents and of the whole affair by a private detective agency hired at college expense. One detective investigated the dissidents' background, visited their former neighborhoods, and talked with their former acquaintances. He also visited Grinnell College in Iowa, which had hired one of the dissidents after his resignation from Parsons, and made charts and drawings "in order that future investigation in this case may be effectively fulfilled." The detective, at least on one occasion, copied a private letter from one of the dissidents to a Parsons faculty member and passed it along to Roberts. But for all of this shabby gumshoeing, the private eye turned up very little of value for his patron.

Roberts's twelve-man committee, however, produced within a week a loose-leaf volume of over 200 pages known as The Green Book or The Green Report, plus a second volume of appendices. The Green Book was made up of data on one or another aspect of the college, signed statements from numerous faculty members, and some comment by the committee itself. It began this way:

> In the statement of the six faculty members . . . many accusations concerning the state of the college were made. Though in some instances hearsay is represented as fact and situations are garbled, much of the material in this statement was commonly known by the faculty and the staff. Much of the material presented as fact is true. The general inferences drawn from these facts we feel to be entirely false.

The report went on to explain that pressures and conflicts and "questionable decisions" were unavoidable when a college was growing at the rate Parsons was, and that "centralized administrative control and responsibility" had been deemed necessary by the Parsons trustees. Roberts, The Green Book admitted, was no angel, but he got things done. If there was sometimes a gap between Roberts's claims and the reality, it was merely an illustration, the committee seemed to say, of a man's reach exceeding his grasp:

> A man of the kind of driving force that could envision the goals as before stated in an environment as little conducive to the realization of such goals is hardly an easy kind of personality to reckon with. To put it simply, he is a hard man to work with and for. He is intemperate when he feels an obstruction is being created that jeopardizes the goals of the College as he sees them. In a situation (without precedent) he shifts policies in various areas, sometimes without notice, when he sees a new method of moving toward his goal. *Since for him intent and action are one and the same, he sometimes states the truth which he is moving toward as the truth which exists as of the present moment.* He tends to brush aside any obstacle he feels is before the realization of College goals in the most direct way possible. This has led to vigor of action on the one hand and expediency on the other. [My italics].

Together The Dissident Report and The Green Book yield a rather full portrait of Parsons as it was in 1963. The first document does pinpoint many of the abuses that persisted at the college throughout Roberts's administration and that increasingly fed the negative reputation of Parsons. But it also suffers from self-righteousness, from a certain pettiness, and from too absolutist and lopsided a view of the college. The other document does describe an institution that has special problems, some extenuating circumstances, but that has to face up to a number of abuses that cannot be explained away. But it suffers from a defensiveness that swings between wounded and belligerent, and from the fact that it does not

try to contest a number of key points in The Dissident Report
—presumably because it was unable to do so.

To some people (not many) the first report would be characterized as an underhanded, conspiratorial attack made out
of personal spite. To some (a great many) the second report
would be a shameless apologia prepared by people under
Roberts's control. If we assume that truth is to be found
somewhere in between these extremes, a reading of the two
reports together affords an excellent insight into the life and
hard times of the college about mid-way through Roberts's
regime. More important for Parsons, however, was the fact
that The Dissident Report was the first time that strong and
detailed criticism of Roberts by insiders had been circulated
not only among some people at the college itself but among
several powerful professional associations outside the college.

Apart from The Dissident Report, however, there was no
substantial dissent from Roberts and his policies on the
campus itself. Certainly there was no sort of organized opposition, as I have said, from the body that would be most expected to offer it, the faculty. For years the Parsons faculty
watched the buccaneering promotionalism of Roberts without
much objection. For years it failed to point out the gap between theory and practice at Parsons and to make clear to
the public and to the educational community at large how far
short the college was falling of its grandiose public pronounce-
ments. For years it suffered Roberts's iron-fisted rule in corporate silence. Tokens of power were thrown to the faculty on
occasion but these concessions, as Harold Eastman, head of
the Parsons sociology department, suggests, meant little. He
recalls this comment from Roberts: "All this is window dress-
ing. You know who's running this place." To be sure, there
were many individuals who quarreled vigorously with Roberts
about one problem or another, and there was continuous
grumbling *sotto voce* among the staff on innumerable issues.

But the plain fact is that the Parsons faculty as a body lacked the courage of its convictions. As a corporate entity, it did not take a strong, unequivocal stand until it was virtually forced to do so by the disaccreditation of the college, after which it formally voted no confidence in Roberts and asked the trustees to fire him. Even then it did so with less than a two-thirds vote; more than one-third of those voting turned down such a resolution.

Still, the faculty *was* starting to show a little muscle in the last year or two of Roberts's administration and possibly would have managed to curb him somewhat if it had been given more time. In August, 1966 the faculty authorized a committee to conduct a sort of self-study of the college to examine "the influence of non-curricular factors on the quality of education at Parsons." This euphemistic mandate was really directed against Roberts and the way he was running the institution. The committee's report, which relied heavily on statements from individual faculty members voluntarily submitted, was presented to the faculty nine months later, after the disaccreditation of Parsons, and was approved.

The report gave strong support to the Parsons Plan, as the faculty had consistently done in the past, but explicitly and implicitly condemned the administration for its methods in carrying it out. The report laid great stress on the importance of honesty and forthrightness in the conduct of all the affairs of the college, and on the importance of establishing a "viable chain of command" at Parsons. It spoke of the "intimidation and harassment" of members of the faculty by the Parsons administrators and in blunt language attacked the credibility, judgment, and competence of the "top administration." Thus the faculty did ultimately go on record as a body, and did so unanimously, against Roberts. Had it done so earlier, much of the Parsons story might have turned out differently.

Parsons and the Church

When Roberts went to Parsons, the college was one of three undernourished Presbyterian colleges in Iowa, the other two being Buena Vista College and the University of Dubuque. In addition, an institution of higher quality, Coe College, maintained informal relations with the church. Parsons operated under a corporate charter that imposed a number of conditions and restraints in exchange for the benefits of church affiliation, including a grant of money each year from the church. One of the conditions was a yearly visit and evaluation by the Board of Visitors. This body had been created in 1953 by the Iowa Synod of the church with the help of the Board of Christian Education, a national arm of the Presbyterian Church. The immediate purpose was to deal with a financial emergency at Buena Vista College. The history of the relations between Roberts and the Board of Visitors is a kind of microcosm of Parsons's relations with the educational world in general.

Things began well enough. The first report of the Board of Visitors after Roberts took over was worried more about the financial problems of the college than about Roberts as an administrator. On the basis of this report, the church decided in December, 1956 to withhold any further payments to Parsons until a comprehensive report by the Board of Visitors could be prepared and such questions as the academic soundness of the college, its economic stability, and the need for a college in the area, could be explored. In October, 1957, two years after Roberts took over, the church received a highly commendatory report on Parsons from the Board of Visitors. In its 1957 visit the Board was particularly impressed by the enrollment increase under Roberts and the consequent reduction of the college debt and thought the future looked promising for the institution and for its relations with the church.

These relations soon began to deteriorate, however, and culminated in disaffiliation five years later. Both the Board of Visitors and the Board of Christian Education of the national church began having doubts about Roberts in 1958 (some individuals even earlier) and the doubts got more serious in 1959. Even at these early dates, the Advisory Committee on Colleges of the Board of Christian Education was so concerned that it several times considered the possibility of the church's severing its ties with Parsons, an action that seemed desirable to E. Fay Campbell, then secretary of the General Division of Higher Education of the national church. Finally in 1960, when conflict between Roberts and the church had reached substantial proportions, the Board of Christian Education appointed a special three-man committee to conduct a full investigation of Parsons—"an investigation," said the church, "to end all investigations."

The three men came from outside Iowa and included Theodore Distler, then executive director of the Association of American Colleges; J. Edward Dirks of the Yale Divinity School; and John D. Moseley, president of Austin College. The eighteen-page report of this committee, submitted to the church in the fall of 1960, is a revealing document. So is the written response that Roberts made to it. Had Roberts abided by both documents, he would have kept out of trouble from that point forward and might well have built himself a much different reputation in American education from the one he wound up with seven years later.

In assessing the college, the special committee tried to take a charitable position while not ignoring the plain facts. It recognized that Parsons under Roberts was "dynamic and vigorous"[10] and that the progress of the preceding five years had been due to "an unorthodox, sometimes ruthless, often indelicate crash program." The committee remarked on what it called Roberts's public relations campaign that had been undertaken along the most studied Madison Avenue lines; unable to begin with the securing of funds, in light of the weakness of the institution, a zealous admissions team implemented the new policy of having the doors thrown open to all students who could be gotten, including those who could not gain entrance to or who had already failed in other colleges; infringements of the rules were winked at in order to keep students in the college; new administrative staff appointments were made in terms of persons of ability who would be loyal to the new President. . . .

The committee praised the faculty for its willingness to take on heavy teaching loads, but urged that the crash program be ended and that endowment and gifts be secured so that Parsons would not be so dependent on student fees. In saying that the college should shift from a public relations campaign of "selling" the president to one that centered on the quality of the instructional program, the committee said, "It is widely recognized now [at Parsons] that this must be done. But this is the more difficult image to project."

The committee recommended a stronger religious program at the college, adding the following comment regarding the reputation of Parsons in the eyes of the church and other church-related colleges even before 1960:

All available studies of the College have come to the Advisory Committee's attention through the Secretary of the Division of Higher Education of the Board of Christian Education. Great patience has been shown; at times, when exasperation with what was reported about the College or its President was unavoidable, it continued to identify itself with the College. This patience has made it possible for the Church not to take precipitous action to sever the ties, even in the face of great uncertainty throughout circles of the Church and the Church-related colleges about whether Parsons College could be "approved" as one of its colleges. However, with rapid developments such as have taken place in the College program, and the vigorous and unorthodox leadership of the present administration, questions, misunderstandings, and a deep sense of mistrust brought about a sense of separation from and even desperation about the College among the leadership and the Advisory Committee of the Division of Higher Education.

Finally, the committee came to grips with the question of Roberts himself:

> . . . the Committee concludes that it is essential that everyone concerned with Parsons College and responsible for its future should confront squarely the question of the College's leadership, so that many of the problems which have been cited may be dealt with constructively. There is the "fact" —well-founded or not, based on prejudice and misunderstanding or not—of an attitude or questioning on the part of many people in the community, in the Church, and in higher education in the area concerning the integrity of the College and its President. Much of this can be explained as misunderstanding and distorted publicity on both sides. Yet, *the fact of the attitude* [italics in original] remains and must be dealt with. . . . This, in all of its ramifications, is almost the central problem of the College.

This special committee report corroborated the views about Parsons that had been building for some years in the General Division of Higher Education of the national church, one of whose leaders upon reading the special report wrote to a friend saying that he could recall meetings "during these trying years" when some people urged that we be patient and see what could be conserved in spite of the very bad things that were happening at Parsons. As I see it now I believe I was wrong about this. It seems to me that it would have been wiser to have forced the issue and demanded that Millard Roberts be dropped some time ago . . . let me say that . . . [Parsons] is one of the most baffling problems we have had to deal with. We want more experimentation in these colleges; we need it. The trouble is there is nothing that I can see in the Parsons picture which tends to enrich higher education or make it more exciting. All the experimentation at Parsons has had to do with how you can get students if you are willing to use certain methods.

Roberts's response to the report of the special committee was astonishingly confessional. He wrote a full apology to the church, acknowledging that he had made "many mistakes" in his crash program, that he still had "a lot to learn," and that he was "sincerely sorry for the mistakes I have made." He promised to abandon the "crash policies" and aim "toward constantly raising the *quality* [his italics] of the entire educational enterprise." He promised to slow down the rate of growth and said that the enrollment would not increase by more than 100 students a year over the next four years, thus "leveling at 2,000 students by 1965." (The actual enrollment in 1965 was 4,304.) Roberts admitted that in his "overweening desire to get things done," he had paid a price in his relations with other people and that he would "measure 'success' from now on in terms of the attitudes of those around me, and not by my own charts and graphs." He also said in regard to his future deportment: "Certainly no crash program is required any more, and my entire area of leadership must center in a quiet, sound pattern of general development, with the stress in the areas of religious emphasis and physical plant."

On the problem of his personal publicity, Roberts asserted that this kind of publicity had given him a lot of trouble, that he didn't really like it and wanted "much less of it." He then added:

If Parsons has made a "notable success" in creating a public relations image in the past five years, for the reasons the [committee] *Report* points out, is it not possible that the same team on my staff can project a much more sincere image of the college itself in the future? My personal desire is to remain at home, do my work, and make as few public appearances as possible. I am more than ready to return to the pattern of an institution carrying the name and the image itself!

Roberts wound up by promising to listen to any further recommendations. He promised to subordinate himself to the trustees, the Board of Visitors, and the church; and, with considerable humility, he expressed the hope that he could continue as president of Parsons.

In the light of this extended *mea culpa, mea maxima culpa,* it would have been sheer churlishness for the church not to take a new and more hopeful view of Parsons. It did, although there were some people in the Board of Christian Education who were not impressed with Roberts's apology and who continued to discuss among themselves, as one of them put it in a report to the Board, "the unsuitability of Dr. Roberts as president . . ." Such *rapprochement* as did occur was short; disenchantment quick. Much of the June, 1960 meeting, for example, between the Parsons administration and the Board of Visitors was concerned with the graduate program that had been announced by Parsons without consultation with the church and which had later been withdrawn under fire, and with "the image of Parsons that has developed over the state."

When it became clear, as it soon did, that Roberts was still energetically on the publicity circuit and that he and the college were going to continue to operate just as they had in the past, relations with the church went into a decline that got rapidly steeper in 1961 and 1962, by which time some of the professional accrediting agencies were finally waking up as well. Parsons's relations with the church reached a crescendo of conflict with the annual visit in 1963 of the Board of Visitors. This visit followed hard upon The Dissident Report that I discussed earlier and on the heels of still another special inspection visit to Parsons by the head of the General Division of Higher Education of the national church. The Board of Visitors had in hand The Dissident Report when it visited Parsons in March of that year, as well as the college's rebuttal (The Green Book), and a record of complaints registered with the Board in previous years. On arrival the Board found a very hostile Roberts, who made it clear that he was in no cooperative mood and would be pleased if they would leave the campus as soon as possible.

In its report that year to the church, the Board of Visitors reviewed the main charges made against Parsons by the dissidents and others and said that it had found many of them true but added that there were some mitigating circumstances for some charges. But it concluded that in the light of all the facts, Parsons should be made to mend its ways or lose its church affiliation. It recommended to the Board of Christian Education that Parsons be put on strict probation for one year while the necessary reforms were effected and that it be dropped by the church at the end of that time if these reforms had not been effected. The Board further suggested, as had the special committee in 1960, that the trustees consider the question of whether the college could be best served in the future by continuing Roberts in the presidency.

One member of the Board of Visitors, however, wrote a minority report taking issue with the Board's analysis and interpretation of the troubles at Parsons. Thus at its annual meeting in June, 1963 the Synod of Iowa (the state division of the national church) contented itself with approving a short statement that expressed its deep concern about Parsons but that also made it clear that reforms would have to take place. It said that "the present situation at Parsons must be corrected if Parsons is to be continued as a church-related college in good standing." The church then offered its services to the Parsons trustees in carrying out the resolution.

The Parsons board of trustees, however, which had been evolving rapidly under Roberts's influence into a more cosmopolitan board than it had been before and with more out-of-state members, reacted quite differently from the way the church hoped. In October, 1963 the Parsons trustees voted to change the articles of incorporation and the bylaws of the college in order to sever its official ties with the church. Parsons took the initiative in making this historic break, not the church as seems to be widely believed. Roberts's reasons, of course, went beyond his feelings that he was constantly being ambushed by the very people who should have been giving him the most support, the church—from which he had regularly received some of the sharpest and most consistent criticism; he also felt that he no longer needed the church and would be glad to be rid of the restraints it imposed on him. Thus Parsons put an end to nearly a century of church affiliation. The Iowa Synod at first sought to compel Parsons by legal means if necessary to maintain its affiliation, but later decided that its best course would be to wait and hope for Roberts's eventual removal and the restoration of Parsons's relationship with the church.

The Reception of Parsons by Outsiders

In previous chapters I have frequently recorded the views of individual outsiders about Parsons and here would add only a few comments about the general reception of the college among people and groups not officially related to Parsons. Among educators the reception changed over time, as it did with the church and most other people. It was marked by curiosity and some uneasiness during the first few years of Roberts's regime but then began to shift to distaste, and in the end turned to severe hostility.

If we are to judge the state of professional thinking by the reports of one of Roberts's private detectives, who deceived a number of educators into talking to her about Roberts and Parsons, their collective opinion by 1963–1964 was strongly negative. Recurrent themes in the detective's interviews were (1) an intense personal animus against Roberts, (2) a belief that Parsons was discrediting all of higher education, (3) a distrust of Parsons's publications and promotional activities, (4) a resentment of the college's making a business out of flunk-outs, (5) a resentment of its raiding other faculties with outlandish salary offers, and (6) an abhorrence of Roberts's unilateral style of government. Perhaps it was all summed up best by Logan Wilson, president of the American Council on Education, when he said to the detective:

It could be that all of us are wrong and Parsons is right. If Parsons is right, then we are all so wrong that we should go out of business. If Parsons is wrong, as I suspect it is, then we owe it to our own dignity and sense of purpose to conduct a formal investigation in the name of all the serious higher education of America.

That some of the professional criticism of Parsons was ill-informed is probably obvious. Relatively few educators outside Parsons knew the institution well. Those who did—and they were mostly paid consultants—took a more hopeful view of the college, though even the consultants found it hard to maintain a consistent enthusiasm for it over time. In a word, Parsons for most of Roberts's tenure fared badly if not always fairly at the hands of American educators in general.

Opinion in the town of Fairfield itself bespoke the sort of division one often finds in small college towns. Before Roberts arrived, Fairfield had had a history of consistent support for the college. The town conducted a yearly drive to raise funds for Parsons and usually presented the college with $25,000 or $30,000 for general support. After Roberts, the local merchants, the chamber of commerce, and householders with rooms to rent continued to support Parsons most of the time, for Roberts was bringing unprecedented amounts of money into the town. But they had their troubles too with the slow-paying college and lost some of their enthusiasm as the institution's local bills piled up.

The attitude of the other residents of Fairfield moved from muted approval in the first few years of Roberts's administration to dislike and even bitterness as the college brought hundreds, then thousands, of new students, many of them wealthy, into a town that itself had only eight or nine thousand people. Local inflation, particularly in the housing market, became a problem, as did the bibulous, high-decibel *bons vivants* from Parsons who roamed the countryside in various kinds of wheeled vehicles.

Walter Williams, publisher of the local paper and a former anti-Roberts trustee, comments, looking back on Roberts's time, that "Parsons College was the main topic of conversation in town. You were either for it or against it. Most people saw no grey area—it was black or white." Another Fairfield resident comments that "this town didn't know when it was well off. They had the goose that laid the golden egg here and all they did was criticize Parsons." On the whole, Fairfield opinion was negative for most of Roberts's career there, a fact that did not escape him. He was right on one point when he said on one occasion, "Nobody ever heard of this hick town before I came, but they don't appreciate that."

So far as the press was concerned, Roberts generally had good luck but with conspicuous exceptions. Regionally he got balanced treatment from the Chicago *Tribune* and good treatment from numerous small papers. Nationally he got good, often laudatory, treatment from news weeklies, radio and television, Sunday supplements, and other publications. Thanks to his public relations firm in New York, he got a free full-page ad in one of the regional issues of *Time* as well as a good deal of other favorable publicity. Over the years he charmed a fair number of reporters who visited Parsons to write about it and who duly reprinted his claims about what was happening there. Even an experienced educational writer like the late David Boroff was taken in by some of the Parsons braggadocio, though in his defense I should add that he did his writing fairly early in Roberts's administration when the propaganda was somewhat easier to believe than it was later on.

One reporter, however, was not taken in, and he was the one who knew the most about the college. James Flansburg of the Des Moines *Register and Tribune* devoted a great deal of time to Parsons, especially in 1965 and 1966, and covered it in a series of interpretive articles as well as regular news columns. He was no admirer of Roberts, a feeling cordially reciprocated. Eventually Flansburg became *persona non grata* at Parsons but could hardly be banned from the campus, where he appeared on one occasion with a bodyguard and a witness in case there was to be litigation. Flansburg did a lot of digging and got a lot of help from people at the college, from some trustees, from former Parsons professors, and from townspeople. His was by far the most penetrating analysis of Parsons done by any reporter during Roberts's administration. His articles were harsh but well-informed. Although they did not give a fully rounded picture of the college, they had justice, for the most part, on their side. They gave Roberts a bad press in one of the places where it counted most: in the state's most widely read newspaper.

The worst single piece of publicity that Roberts ever received was an article in *Life* called "The Wizard of Flunk-Out U," which appeared in the June 3, 1966 issue. It was the work of members of *Life*'s Chicago staff and had been done with the encouragement of a Milwaukee public relations firm that Roberts was then retaining. Both Roberts and his publicists expected treatment that would be favorable in the customary way. The article, enriched with large photographs and plentiful quotes from Parsons's students, turned out to be a racy, satirical, and blistering account of Roberts's "rip-roaring, bell-ringing, every-time-a-bulls-eye salesmanship and rigid cost accounting." The main focus of the piece was on the country-club aspect of the college, the draft-dodging "dumb rich kids," the sports cars, the hard-drinking party-goers, and the fat profit that Parsons said it was making out of it all.

Roberts was understandably enraged by this article, as were the faculty and the students. They felt, and still feel today, that it was designed to cast the worst possible light on the college. They allege that, as one student put it, "That reporter dragged out every slob he could find around here," and that the total impression left by the article was that Parsons was hopelessly, if comically, caught in the grip of greed, booze, and depravity.

Fairfield itself was no less incensed, feeling that the article was a savage attack on the whole community. It launched a "Fairfield Fights Back" campaign financed by gifts to try to refute the story, although it is not clear whether the Fairfield-fight-back idea originated with the town or the public relations firm. "It was," said the chairman of the campaign, "as if a bomb had been dropped on our town—every citizen has been stunned by the insinuations, innuendoes, and slanted half-truths. . . . Parsons College is a part of our community and we'll fight for it." Fairfield collected all the old and new *Life*'s it could find, paying a nickel each for them, in order to sell them for scrap paper and, as a gesture, give the proceeds to Parsons for a *"Life"* scholarship. Residents even went around town with simulated black eyes to symbolize the victimization of the town by the magazine. The campaign soon fizzled out, however, when the Parsons trustees and townspeople realized that it was only calling further attention to a situation that might best be left to simmer down and die.

In my own view the *Life* article was not as bad as Parsons, understandably enough, thought it was, and would have been less damaging if the college had said nothing. It was written in the idiom of tongue-in-cheek popular journalism, the object being to amuse rather than enlighten. It did not tell the whole story of Parsons by a wide margin, but it did present one segment of it in rather caricatured form. And after all, there may well have been a certain wry justice in the whole episode. In view of the number of other reporters who had been conned by Parsons in previous years, perhaps the conning of Parsons by *Life* was merely just retribution.

In any case, the article, aided or not by the Parsons-Fairfield reaction to it, had consequences. Parsons claimed that it was responsible for reducing that summer's enrollment, and even more the next fall's enrollment. The college estimated that it lost 500 students in the fall of 1966 because of the article, which meant over $1 million in revenue that the college had been expecting but did not get. Even more important were the article's indirect consequences. It caused the regional accrediting association to take steps that ended in disaster for both Roberts and the college—victims, in a way, of their own overblown publicity.

NOTES

[1] *Phi Delta Kappan* (June, 1968), p. 590.

[2] *The Operating Plan of Parsons College from 1965 to 1980,* a document signed by Roberts and released in April, 1966.

[3] From a speech called "College Admissions and the National Purpose" (November 5, 1962).

[4] *An Analysis of Parsons Students in Graduate Schools,* a report issued by Parsons (April 20, 1963).

[5] From an undated speech called, "Better Education for Less Money."

[6] See Allan M. Cartter, ed., *American Universities and Colleges* (Washington, D.C.: American Council on Education, 1964); *The Handbook of the Association of College Admissions Counselors* (1967–1970 edition); James Cass and Max Birnham, *Comparative Guide to American Colleges* (New York: Harper & Row, 1965); and *Barron's Profiles of American Colleges* (1967).

[7] From a recruiting leaflet called "Parsons—the College for *You.*"

[8] "Parsons Graduates During the Last Decade" (June, 1964).

[9] Archie R. Dykes, "Faculty Participation in Academic Decision Making," ACE (1968), p. 38.

[10] Quotations from the special committee report and Roberts's response are made by permission of the Board of Christian Education of the Presbyterian Church.

7: Adventures in Accreditation

The world is ruled by force, not by opinion; but opinion uses force.

—PASCAL

Power is so apt to be insolent, and liberty so saucy, that they are very seldom on good terms.

—MARQUIS OF HALIFAX

Who will stand guard over the guards themselves?

—JUVENAL

Like a balky, worrisome teen-ager who wants his freedom from home but is dependent on home for survival, Parsons alternately resisted and importuned the North Central Association of Colleges and Secondary Schools (NCA); and the NCA alternately indulged and chastised this most difficult member of its very extensive family. NCA is the largest of six regional accrediting associations that together blanket the United States and its territories, acting as regulatory and stimulative agencies. They visit and evaluate both secondary schools and colleges and admit to membership those institutions that meet certain standards and criteria. They examine and approve the entire institution rather than one or another segment or program of it, as does a specialized accrediting agency, and they publish lists of their member institutions for the guidance of other schools and colleges, government bodies, foundations, and the general public. It is this general stamp of approval that most people have in mind when they ask whether an institution is "fully accredited."

The six regional accrediting associations are nongovernmental bodies that came into being in the last century as a means of insuring some degree of standardization or comparability among the myriad of educational institutions that then operated with few restrictions throughout the country. Because of the political decentralization of the United States, the federal government has never attempted to fill the educational policing role that is filled in other countries by the central government, either through a ministry of education or some special body such as Britain's University Grants Committee. Instead it has been the private "voluntary associations" of schools and colleges—the regional accrediting associations —that have given us such regulation and surveillance as we have had.

For institutions that are already members, the regionals send in visiting teams of examiners at widely spaced intervals to make an assessment that almost without exception reaffirms the institution's accreditation. The regionals are permissive associations that let in large numbers of institutions of dubious quality. They are not known for disciplining their members very harshly and they practically never throw anybody out. Parsons was an exception to these rules, as it was to so many others. The rather tortuous history of Parsons's relations with NCA was as much a test of NCA as it was of Parsons. Unfortunately both flunked.

A Rash of Accreditation Visits

Normally the NCA conducts a formal re-evaluation at ten-year intervals (and often at even longer intervals) of schools that are already members. With Parsons, however, it sent no fewer than four official visiting teams to the campus within the space of eight years during Roberts's administration (in

1959, 1963, 1964, and 1967). Add to that two more official visits after the departure of Roberts, one in 1968 and another one scheduled for 1970, and we have no fewer than six full-scale assessments of Parsons College within an eleven-year period. There can be few schools anywhere in the country that have been evaluated by supposedly expert examiners as often as Parsons. If the NCA still does not know as much as it should about Parsons—and it doesn't—it ought to look to the adequacy of its methods of evaluation.

Four of the five visiting teams that went to Parsons between 1959 and 1968 filed reports with NCA that were on the whole favorable to the college and that recommended favorable action by NCA. Unfortunately, I cannot quote from or reprint any of these reports, except the 1967 report which was released to the press by Parsons. NCA policy prohibits the reprinting of team reports without permission of the institution involved, and NCA practice frowns on it at any time. At a meeting with the executive committee of the Parsons board of trustees in 1968, I requested permission to reprint all or parts of the NCA reports but was turned down. Parsons at that time was in pursuit of reaccreditation and was exceedingly anxious to do nothing to offend NCA. I think the college would be well advised at some point in the future when it feels secure in its relations with NCA to publish all six reports and get them out on the public record. But meanwhile, we will have to be content with a brief summary of them.

The first NCA visit during Roberts's administration came in 1959 after several years of publicity that had raised doubts in the minds of many educators and had raised the temperatures of quite a few. The 1959 report, however, praised most of what had been done at Parsons. It spoke highly of the trustees and of Roberts's dynamic leadership while also noting that he had his critics on the campus. It found little to quarrel with in the academic program or the building program. Its most unfavorable comments were made on the low admissions standards of Parsons, on the low performance standards of students already on the campus, and on Parsons's hard-sell recruiting and publicity operations. However, the final impression left by the report was quite positive, and Parsons's accreditation was therefore reaffirmed by NCA.

Things changed rapidly over the next few years. The deficiencies pointed to in 1959 got worse. Parsons's press-agentry got noisier; its relations with the church reached the breaking point; and its reputation among educators declined further. If Roberts had chosen to work *with* NCA during these years, as he would have had he been half the politician that people give him credit for being, his accreditation troubles would have been avoided; but that kind of cooperation never took place. Finally in March, 1963 came the internal eruption of The Dissident Report, which was sent to NCA after it had first been sent to the trustees and the church. The Dissident Report seemed to confirm the worst fears of outside educators, including those who had already been putting pressure on NCA to do something about Parsons. NCA immediately sent in a team of visitors.

In one of my talks with Roberts, he told me that the 1963 NCA team had been composed of "three Iowa college presidents who were embarrassed by a college in their state without a deficit." In fact the 1963 team was made up of five people, all of them from outside Iowa and only one of them a college president. They spent two days at Parsons and wrote a scathing thirty-two page indictment of Roberts and the college. Although they found some good things to say about such matters as Parsons's finances and the quality of the faculty, their negative comments—expressed in a surprisingly emotional idiom—were far stronger and more frequent.

They came down hard, again, on Parsons's recruiting and promotional activities; on the primacy of financial considerations in the making of educational policy; on the lack of accurate statistics and reliable institutional research; on

Roberts's domination of the faculty; on the turnover of faculty members; on the heavy teaching load; and in particular on the failure of the college to do what it publicly boasted it was doing in the way of rescuing late bloomers and flunk-outs from other colleges. The team accused the college of failing to provide the kind of guidance and counseling it advertised and of failing to maintain respectable standards (which remained undefined by the team) for grades and degrees—in brief, for not doing what it said it was doing. It was a devastating report.

On the basis of this document, the NCA executive board decided two months later, apparently by a vote of five to three, to put Parsons on probation, saying that another full-scale visit would be made the next academic year to determine if the college had rectified the "grave weaknesses" uncovered, and, if it had not, to consider disaccreditation. NCA invented a new category of probation for Parsons, called "public probation," so that it could issue a public warning against the college. Roberts was convinced that NCA was more worried about him than about the "grave weaknesses" of the college, or perhaps thought of him as the gravest weakness, and that a conspiracy to "get" him had taken place involving NCA, the church, and other groups and individuals (although Parsons's private detectives were inconclusive on the point). He considered suing NCA, as he had considered suing the six dissidents, but thought better of it on advice of counsel. Instead he gave some thought to setting up an accrediting agency of his own while at the same time moving to meet the NCA complaints.

The next visit came in December, 1964, having been postponed from the previous academic year to give Roberts and some of his new administrators time to make the necessary changes. Parsons this time got a good report which recommended removal of probation. The visiting team found most of the 1963 complaints answered, or thought they did. They commented favorably on the quality and the salaries of the faculty and did not mention the faculty turnover rate (which was still very high); they commented favorably on such aspects of the Parsons Plan as the trimester system, the restricted curriculum, and team teaching. They found improvements in the administrative structure and in the authority exercised by the faculty (which was still just as much or little as Roberts wanted to part with).

Once again, however, they commented on the need for accurate data and institutional research, and on the harmful reputation that Parsons, through its uninhibited promotionalism, was building in educational circles. The visiting team in a conference with Roberts and some of his advisers before leaving the campus made a special effort to impress on Roberts the importance of his telling the whole truth about Parsons's finances. Roberts promised at that meeting to stop using the word *profit* in his promotional activities and to start emphasizing the educational instead of the financial aspects of the college. The team went away more or less happy. In 1965 NCA removed Parsons from probation on the basis of this report, with the provision that still another visit would be made within three years.

Looking back on that period of Parsons's history, one of the new administrators brought in by Roberts to help meet NCA complaints recalls that

> I spent weeks on the road trying to get us off probation. I talked to everybody, asking for a second chance for Parsons, saying we now had a good faculty, etc. They agreed to give us the chance. Roberts then proceeded to do everything the opposite of what he said we would do. I don't see how you can give a guy like that another chance.

In the two years that intervened between the removal of Parsons's probation and the next visit from NCA, Roberts

carried on much as he had before, only with more of everything: more students, more staff, more money, more administrators, and more publicity. It was during these years that
Roberts also got his satellite colleges started (with Parsons's
funds and with himself as a paid consultant to them), a movement that was seen as a deadly threat by many other colleges.
William Munson, vice president for academic affairs at the
time of disaccreditation and later acting president, comments
this way:

> Once Roberts got off NCA probation he felt he could go
> full steam ahead with his publicity. The worst mistake he
> made was to invade the state education systems. I told him,
> "You are making a terrible error having the whole Wiscon-
> sin delegation down here. Why do you want to go down
> into Mississippi? Why do you want to mess up the Okla-
> homa system? Why invade the Wisconsin system? Why go
> on Art Linkletter's program? Why get on Mike Douglas's
> program and why get on the Huntley-Brinkley program
> and have them out here? What you are going to do is to
> make NCA and other administrators so mad they will dis-
> accredit this place and get you."

Munson's prophetic soul was right. The crunch came with
the *Life* article that I discussed in Chapter 6 and the damaging publicity it created for Parsons. "The administration,"
says a Parsons trustee, "generated this kind of publicity
through thoughtless actions and an unerring ability not to
read warning signals." Two months after the *Life* article, NCA
announced that it would send another visiting team to Parsons
within a few months. That decision brought a sharp objection
from one of NCA's own consultants who had been working
with Parsons since the previous NCA visit, a letter that I will
reprint later. It is not clear whether the *Life* article actually
disturbed NCA so much that it precipitately decided to mount

another visit to Parsons or whether NCA was already determined to do something about the college but lacked an
excuse to schedule a visit until *Life* supplied it.

In any event, NCA's fourth team in eight years made its
visit in February, 1967. It produced a thirty-two-page report
that recommended, to the surprise of practically everybody
when it became known later, "reaffirmation of accreditation"
but with the proviso that Parsons agree to continue with an
NCA consultant and to make quarterly reports to NCA. The
team found many improvements since 1964 and reinforced
many of the commendatory observations of the 1964 report.
It spoke highly of the counseling service, of the quality of the
faculty, of the faculty's participation in decisions (though
noting that further improvement was still needed), and of
the team teaching and trimester system.

But it also found a great deal wrong. It felt the curriculum
was too narrow, that remedial courses in certain subjects were
needed, that faculty turnover was high, that the student-
faculty ratio was bad, that Parsons was growing too fast, that
its financial condition was precarious (the first NCA team to
take this position), that it needed more gifts and less reliance
on tuition income, and that its budgeting process was very
poor. Once more, the team also came down hard on the
Parsons "image," saying:

> Parsons College operates within the framework of a credi-
> bility gap. There is both an internal credibility gap and an
> external credibility gap. The internal credibility gap re-
> mains because there is a carelessness in the use of statistical
> information and a tendency to engage in excessive exaggera-
> tion. . . . A determined effort must be made by the college
> to bring accuracy to the reports of the college so that in-
> tegrity of information will be beyond question. One of the
> historical purposes of all institutions of higher education is
> to seek and protect truth. The careless manner in which

some members of the college administration use statistical information promotes and reinforces the internal credibility gap.

On the other, there is an external credibility gap in which members of the academic community at large are willing to believe rumors and exaggerated reports about Parsons College often without due regard to the strength of the internal program as it exists.

The team found the overcrowding of the Parsons dormitories a serious problem but also that student morale was improving:

Although the college may not view it as such, in our opinion the *Life* Magazine article of last year has had a favorable impact on the campus atmosphere. There is a growing interest in and commitment to Parsons College as an institution on the part of the students. They are developing a pride in it. This atmosphere carries over to the faculty and there is a feeling on the campus that Parsons College may really be in the midst of a landmark experiment in higher education for America.

And once more, the team complained, as had all three previous teams, about inadequate institutional research at Parsons and about the lack of reliable data. One member of the team wrote that he

was told [by Parsons] that commonly recognized definitions of basic statistics did not exist, so that no single official enrollment figure is used. Data on retention and dropout of students were very fuzzy and represented several combined types. . . . In summary, it appears that some progress is being made in the development of a basic data system, but not as much as would have been expected under the circumstances. There is still evidence of lack of concern about the consistency and reliability of data and the consistency of use of data. . . . Whether it is intentional or not, the provision of statistics that combine several groups—in reporting attrition statistics, in reporting SAT scores, and in reporting financial income and expenditures—can only serve to confuse and provide a fuzzy picture of the institution and what it is actually doing. In some instances, at least, this fuzziness appears to cover up what might be considered to be major deficiencies of the institution. The net combination of fuzzy statistics and the distorted use in the reporting of statistics makes it extremely difficult to be sure just where the institution does stand.

In spite of these considerable strictures, some of which were not justified as I will mention later, the report of the 1967 team taken in the round was favorable. On the basis of the team's conversations at Parsons before leaving the campus, everybody felt confident of a good recommendation to NCA. But six weeks after the visit, Roberts received this letter from NCA:

This is to inform you officially that the North Central Association, at its meeting on April 6, 1967, voted to drop Parsons College from its list of member institutions, effective June 30, 1967. This action was taken on the basis of the examination report which recognized certain elements of improvement, but found that other major deficiencies, as reflected in the examiners' report, had not been corrected. It was because of the persistent failure of the College to correct these serious weaknesses that the North Central Association voted to drop the institution from membership in the Association.

At a meeting of the faculty a few days after this bomb had been dropped, Roberts expressed complete bewilderment at

NCA's action. He did not understand, he said, what the "persistent weaknesses" were or why they had not been made plain to him—as indeed they had not—at a meeting that he and other Parsons administrators had had with NCA shortly before the disaccreditation (although a reading of the four NCA team reports would have told anybody what the weaknesses were). He then reviewed defensively the college's relations with NCA over the years saying that the first report (1959) had found that Parsons was a nice little college doing well and had made no suggestions for change (in fact the 1959 report made a number of suggestions for change, including one for toning down certain specific pages of the catalogue).

Roberts then said that the famous 1963 report which had caused Parsons to be put on probation, could then be read by anybody (it had been kept secret up to that point); and added, incredibly, that the material of that report had not been related to the NCA decision to put Parsons on probation, implying that the decision had been arbitrary and premeditated and not supported by the report. I don't know whether the probation was premeditated or not, but no outsider could read the detailed and strongly condemnatory 1963 report and believe that it had nothing to do with the NCA decision. Roberts then said that the 1964 report which had got Parsons off probation had not made any recommendations for change. That again is an interpretation that probably no other person reading that report could come to, for it did make a considerable number of suggestions, both general and specific, for change at Parsons.

Roberts then commented on some of the criticisms of Parsons in the 1967 report but not on the most important ones. He added that Parsons was spending from $30,000 to $60,000 a year for consultants who were supposed to tell the college whether it was doing the right or the wrong things and help to avoid such catastrophes as disaccreditation; he had telephoned them, he said, to ask why this calamity had over-taken Parsons, and they had suggested that maybe he needed some more consultants.

How much justice there was in the attitude taken by Roberts and Parsons that NCA had never made clear to them just what the "persistent weaknesses" were or how the college could have been disaccredited on the basis of the 1967 report, and how much justice there was in NCA's decision, are compli-cated questions that I will return to presently. First we need to look at some of the immediate consequences of the dis-accreditation.

The Trustees Fire Roberts and Take NCA to Court

"Depend upon it, sir," said Dr. Johnson, "when a man knows he is to be hanged in a fortnight, it concentrates his mind wonderfully." Maybe so, but disaccreditation seems to have created more chaos than concentration at Parsons. Over the next three months a kind of *opera bouffe* took place. Should the college seek reconciliation or confrontation with NCA? Should Roberts quit or forge aggressively ahead? Should he be fired or supported, or made a figurehead? Should the faculty support or condemn the administration? Should the trustees support the faculty or Roberts? Should worried parents and students be disarmed or warned about the con-sequences of disaccreditation? People wound up at different times wanting to do all of these things and sometimes doing conflicting things simultaneously.

First the college filed a formal appeal with NCA. Then the student senate of Parsons met and passed a resolution showing that the students had been unified rather than disaffected from Parsons by the disaccreditation:

We feel that the North Central Association is unfair, first, because the reasons for loss of accreditation are not specific enough in the report to warrant such action. Further, we feel it is unfair to the students in particular and the college in general because disaccreditation implies that we are not learning as much at Parsons as we would at an accredited college. We do not accept this implication.

Finally, we the students of Parsons College, wish to proclaim our full faith in and unconditional support of our institution.

Then the faculty met and passed a resolution pledging support for the Parsons system and for everybody in the Parsons community "from Trustees through students" in pursuit of their common goal of reaccreditation.

A short time after that a group of eight members of the faculty Professional Problems Committee appeared before the trustees to make a formal presentation on behalf of the faculty to the effect that Roberts was the cause of all the trouble. This group reviewed with the trustees the history of turmoil at Parsons, the desire of the faculty for more authority than it had, the validity of some of NCA's criticisms, the problem of the credibility gap, and the desire of the faculty to avoid legal action that might throw all of the institution's dirty linen into the public wash basin. It was an effort by a desperate faculty to apprise the trustees of what had really been happening on the campus over a period of years. The Trustees responded very positively to this presentation, which apparently opened the eyes of some of them.

Two weeks later the faculty, in a divided, free-swinging, and often bitter meeting, reversed its earlier position, voted a resolution of no confidence in Roberts, and asked the board of trustees to fire him. The vote was 101 to 58. It was a revealing meeting for some faculty members in that personal complaints against Roberts and other administrators which had been coming for years to the Professional Problems Committee were openly discussed along with other kinds of information not before available to the full faculty.

Many of those who disagreed with the faculty resolution did so on the ground that the Parsons Plan could not operate effectively without Roberts and that his departure would only insure the bankruptcy of the college. Others felt that the faculty by this action was forcing the hand of the trustees who, as was widely rumored on the campus, had every intention of easing Roberts out in any event and had been moving in that direction for the last year. Still others felt that the resolution would have the opposite of the hoped-for effect on NCA and, far from getting a reconsideration for Parsons, would solidify NCA's determination to make the disaccreditation stick. And at least a few felt that the whole affair was being engineered by people who wanted Roberts's job.

The trustees for their part were not pleased with the faculty vote, which had been released to the press, or with other out-of-channels activities of the faculty. At their regular June commencement meeting two weeks later, they passed a resolution of their own unanimously expressing their displeasure with members of the faculty who had been bypassing the administration and going directly to one or another trustee with complaints and who had also violated the college bylaws by going directly to NCA to bargain. At the same time, however, the trustees realized that they could no longer postpone some kind of action. At one point in the meeting a motion was made requiring Roberts to turn in his resignation on the spot and the trustees to accept it on the spot, but after some discussion that motion was withdrawn.

The trustees then put a special committee of the board to work in another room on the NCA problem. There was extended discussion in this committee as to whether Roberts's resignation was necessary for the college to regain its accreditation and if so how much compensation would have to be paid to Roberts and his wife to meet contractual obligations. The minutes of this meeting, which were later introduced in court, said in part:

> A considerable number of members of the Committee, other Trustees, and some staff members as well as a majority of the Faculty felt that accreditation by the North Central Association should be saved *at any price* [italics in the original]. This belief would, of course, include the request for the resignation of the President of the College, if that would achieve the desired end.

The committee therefore recommended that the trustees plan to meet again on June 27, immediately after Parsons's appeal was scheduled to be considered and decided upon by NCA, after which one of three courses of action was to be taken. First, if the appeal was granted, Roberts would quit and receive full compensation for his contract. Second, if NCA said no, Roberts would stay and the college would sue NCA. Third, if neither NCA nor the courts gave Parsons relief, Roberts would also stay "because the needs of the College in that situation would be very great. . . ." It was a curious trio of alternatives, as C. Clyde Wright, a strong supporter of Roberts and chairman of the board of trustees, indicated:

> Mr. Wright pointed out that he did not hold accreditation as worth getting *at any price,* including the sacrificing of the President of the College who had done so much to build it. It was strange, he said, to have a policy position on accreditation which called for sacrificing the President in one situation, and saying that his leadership was essential in two other possible situations.

Even more curious if not comical was the trustees' decision to make NCA aware of these alternatives and to try to strike a bargain with NCA in which the trustees offered Roberts's head in exchange for accreditation. The idea was that Roberts would write out his resignation and give it to the chairman of the board of trustees. Then he, the chairman, and a third man who was to become acting president of Parsons if Roberts left, were to attend a special meeting of the NCA executive board on June 14 to see if NCA would make a bargain. The most curious thing of all would have been if NCA, no matter how much it might have relished having Roberts's head offered to it on a platter, had made a deal. "I had Roberts's resignation in my pocket," says Wright, "when I went to the NCA meeting but they didn't even ask to see it." Of course NCA could not agree to such a course, but there are many people who think it would have been glad to make the trade if the trustees had in fact fired Roberts first without conferring with them. Raymond Gibson, provost of Parsons at the time, comments that

> The trustees had made a motion to fire Roberts but could not get a majority. If they had, the June 14 meeting of NCA would probably have restored accreditation. The reason NCA [later] turned down the appeal is that the college had worked out this reprehensible deal to trade Roberts's resignation for accreditation.

That scheme having failed, the next step was taken by a group of seven senior faculty members of Parsons who at the eleventh hour tried to sell an idea of their own to NCA that had some similarities to the one dreamed up by the trustees. On June 22, two days before NCA was to make its decision on Parsons's appeal, they took a statement to NCA that seemed to say Roberts was on his way out in any case and that they hoped NCA would amend its attitude toward Parsons accordingly. The statement read:

It is now abundantly clear that Parsons College cannot survive for even a one-year period unless accreditation is regained. Though the majority of the faculty is sufficiently dedicated to the basic concepts which underlie the program at Parsons to remain at the college even though a few lean years might be involved, it is quite clear that their doing so is contingent upon the college's regaining accreditation. Very few if any of the existing faculty would elect to remain in the absence of academic as distinct from legal accreditation even if the financial future of the college were assured.

The faculty in its May 24, 1967 vote of no confidence in the Administration of the College manifested its conviction that drastic changes in the management of the College were imperative. Faculty experience at Parsons has provided convincing proof that the required changes in the management of the College cannot be achieved so long as the present chief executive remains in office. Though other changes in administrative personnel are also unquestionably necessary, the initial step in modifying and redirecting the management of the College's affairs cannot be taken until the chief administrator is removed from office.

Most of the faculty and most of the members of the executive committee of the college's governing board recognize, as the 1967 NCA visitation team report indicates, that administrative policies and practices are in desperate need of a major overhaul.

Most of the faculty and most of the members of the executive committee of the Board of Trustees also recognize that the necessary first step in accomplishing the overhaul is the removal from office of the current President of the College.

The internal politics of the governing board are such that, though inevitable within a few months, removal of the President from office cannot be accomplished, in all probability, by 1 July 1967.

In exchange for a pledge from the faculty and the Board of Trustees to proceed forthwith to the task of effecting appropriate changes in the College's administrative policies and practices we respectfully request that accreditation be restored contingent upon a reasonable probationary period during which credible progress can be accomplished and shown.

On June 24 the NCA board of directors met and considered Parsons's formal appeal, which had been filed earlier, as well as the propositions that had been put to it by the trustees and the faculty. It voted unanimously to deny the appeal. The Parsons executive committee met immediately thereafter and, instead of following the course of action approved by the trustees ten days earlier in case of an NCA denial, reversed itself and fired Roberts. Not only did they fire him, but they did so without compensation, accusing him of having breached his contract with the trustees and of a variety of specific offenses. The trustees abrogated Roberts's contract as of the end of the month and required him to vacate the presidential house forthwith. The firing of Roberts may have seemed to many people a very long time in coming, but when it came it turned out to be one of the most summary sackings in the annals of higher education.

Barnaby Keeney, former president of Brown University, commented a decade ago on the office of the college president this way:

Actually, the office depends upon confidence, just as the position of a prime minister in a parliamentary democracy depends on confidence. The president cannot make the

trustees do anything; he cannot make the alumni do anything; he cannot make the public do anything; he cannot
make the faculty do anything, though he can stop them
from doing anything; and good students are notably impervious to direct orders. He can, however, cause these
people to do a great deal, and, if he is a good president he
does; but whether he is or not depends upon their daily
vote of confidence. When the president loses the confidence
of a sufficient number of these constituencies, he ceases to
be effective and should either resign or be removed.[1]

Whether or not one thinks that the Parsons presidency was
conducted on that rather high plane, what is certain is that
by the end of June, 1967 Roberts had lost the confidence of
practically all of his "constituencies."

William Munson, who became acting president after
Roberts's departure, recalls his earlier attempt to persuade
Roberts to resign as gracefully as possible:

We could not have made peace with the NCA without
Roberts resigning. If he had been a great man, he would
have seen this. I asked him why he did not resign and
perhaps the board would give him very good treatment. . . .
I said this in May after the NCA action in April. He replied "If I resign, it will appear that those bastards up there
in Chicago have got me. I can't do it and I won't do it."

My argument was altruistic because I said to him, "As
long as you are president, there is not a dog's chance of
ever getting reaccredited." He said, "You can't be sure of
that." I said, "I am as certain as I can be. For the good of
the place, why don't you resign?"

Ward Hunt, one of the Parsons trustees from Fairfield who
had been a Roberts supporter, recalls the situation this way:

Up to the loss of accreditation the board was 100 per cent behind Roberts—the program was going along well, the financial progress looked very optimistic. Then when accreditation was withdrawn, it was a shock to everybody. It brought out all the dirty linen. There evidently had been quite a smoldering resentment in the faculty. Roberts had been a little Napoleon. The board knew a little of this but thought it was not serious as long as he was doing his job.

There was a bit more than that to the firing of Roberts but suffice it to say that on June 26 the following actions were taken at the meeting of the Parsons executive committee: The executive committee of the board of trustees fired Roberts in the fashion I have indicated, whereupon the chairman of the board also quit; the trustees appointed Munson acting president; and they decided to sue NCA to prevent Parsons's disaccreditation. Parsons's lawyers immediately filed a complaint in Federal District Court in Chicago (NCA headquarters) seeking a preliminary injunction that would require NCA to retain Parsons on its accredited list until a full trial could be held on the merits of the case.

The college charged that NCA's attempted disaccreditation was "biased, unjust, arbitrary, oppressive, lacking in good faith, and contrary to natural justice." It charged NCA with a violation of "rudimentary due process" and said the NCA bylaws did not adequately define standards and procedures so as to afford elementary protection to its members. The college further claimed that it had not been given adequate notice at any time that its accreditation was in jeopardy, had never been presented with a statement of charges to which it could respond, and had had no opportunity to confront its accusers. Finally, it claimed that the standards by which it was judged were nebulous and vague, that enormous financial harm had already been done to the college and that more would be done if the disaccreditation were allowed to stand.

However, a few weeks after filing this complaint, after still further conferences with NCA, and after court proceedings on the preliminary injunction sought by Parsons had nearly been completed, the trustees decided to withdraw their suit. They had been led to believe by NCA, or at least thought they had, that Parsons's chances of keeping its accreditation would be enhanced if they stopped the litigation. So they decided to seek reconciliation with NCA instead of fighting it in court. If NCA *did* give such assurances or suggestions to the Parsons trustees, it is hard to see why that kind of trade is any more defensible than the one offered NCA earlier by the trustees. But the Parsons lawyers were unable to effect withdrawal of the suit in time to prevent publication of the court's opinion.

The hearing on Parsons's motion for a preliminary injunction was held in July, 1967 and produced a number of interesting documents and exhibits along with 500 pages of transcript. In order to get a favorable decision, Parsons was faced with the job of persuading the court, in this case Judge Julius Hoffman, of its charges against NCA to such a degree as to indicate probable success if the case were to go to actual trial. But Parsons was in the awkward position of attacking the bylaws as inadequate and the standards of evaluation as nebulous of an association that it had voluntarily joined and in which it now wanted to remain.

Of course, a college that disapproved in advance of the bylaws and standards would still have little choice but to join its regional accrediting association in order to survive and prosper, but that is not an impressive argument or one that lends itself to proof in a court of law. Parsons was also in the position of having to prove probable bias and arbitrariness on the basis of one or another document such as the 1967 visiting team report which, whatever its deficiencies, did not lend itself readily to that kind of analysis.

Among the legal precedents cited by the college was one involving the expulsion of a doctor from a voluntary medical association, a case won by the doctor when the court decided that "If expulsion from a voluntary association is without rudimentary due process, that expulsion is invalid and may be voided by the court." But in the Parsons case, the court decided that "rudimentary due process" had been observed by NCA. In deciding against the college, the court admitted that Parsons had proved abundantly well the financial and other damage involved in its disaccreditation, but added that "even the greatest hardship . . . will not support the issuance of a preliminary injunction if the defendant has committed no legal or equitable wrong." The court decided that NCA had not committed either a "legal or equitable wrong"; that no violation of bylaws had been proved or any arbitrary disregard by NCA of its own established procedures; or that NCA had failed to give the college an adequate hearing. However, the court declined to evaluate NCA's standards themselves or its internal procedures, or the adequacy of its reasons for disaccrediting the college:

In this field, the courts are traditionally even more hesitant to intervene. The public benefits of accreditation, dispensing information and exposing misrepresentation, would not be enhanced by judicial intrusion. Evaluation by the peers of the college, enabled by experience to make comparative judgments, will best serve the paramount interest in the highest practicable standards in higher education. The price for such benefits is inevitably some injury to those who do not meet the measure, and some risk of conservatism produced by appraisals against a standard of what has already proven valuable in education.

In short, the court said that a voluntary association should be allowed to make its own rules and carry on its own business without interference from the courts as long as ordinary due process is observed. Parsons failed to make a sufficiently strong showing that it had been deprived of due process to get its preliminary injunction. Thereafter the trustees dropped the whole suit, though they were not required to do so. Thus the Parsons case was never brought to trial on its merits and one can only speculate on what a court's decision might be if such an expulsion case were ever to be tried.

There are those who hold that the case was badly handled, that there should have been additional charges made such as unequal application of the laws, and that the complaint should have been filed in Federal District Court in Iowa, which might have been a friendlier jurisdiction, instead of Illinois. Even after defeat at the federal level in Illinois, there were those, such as acting president Munson, who wanted to reinstate the suit in the state courts and to do it on antitrust grounds. But no amount of hindsight could affect the basic situation of the college: it had already suffered enormous damage and faced a good deal more, had attracted even more unfavorable publicity than usual, had been unable to redress its grievances in court, and had no realistic choice left to it but to seek reaccreditation through normal channels.

Thus Parsons became one of only three institutions in our history to put up a court fight against those powerful bodies, the regional accrediting associations. The first such suit, in 1938, was also brought against NCA. It was brought by the governor of North Dakota on behalf of the state university, which had been disaccredited by NCA. This case was also lost by the college when the court decided that it had not exhausted its remedies within NCA (it had not filed an appeal with NCA), but also, and secondarily, because, as the court said: "Voluntary associations have the right to make their own regulations as to admission or expulsion of members, and one who becomes a member, by its membership assents to the constitution and rules of procedure adopted by the association."

So just as the court did in the Parsons case, this federal court also took seriously the claim of the regionals that they are voluntary associations. However, the issue of whether they are really voluntary and whether such associations do indeed have the right to make their "own regulations as to admission" was the subject of the third and most recent lawsuit against a regional association. In March, 1969 the suit of Marjorie Webster Junior College, a proprietary (profit-making) college in the District of Columbia, against the Middle States Association (the regional accrediting body that covers the District) went to trial. Middle States, in company with the other five regionals around the country, restricts its membership to non-profit institutions and had therefore always refused to visit, evaluate, or accredit Marjorie Webster Junior College.

The college based its suit on two principal grounds: (1) that Middle States was a monopoly in unreasonable restraint of trade within the meaning of the antitrust laws; and (2) that Middle States was performing various kinds of functions on behalf of, and essential to, government agencies; and was therefore, as a quasi-governmental body, subject to the restraints of the Constitution—including the observance of due process and the avoidance of arbitrary or unreasonable actions such as prohibiting, without a hearing or an examination, membership to proprietary institutions.

The case was complex and the trial long. The trial transcript runs to 7,311 pages accompanied by numerous depositions and some hundreds of exhibits and other documents. These records together with those of the Parsons case constitute a unique body of information about regional accrediting in the United States, a subject that, in my view, is badly in need of a thorough critical study. If and when such a study is made, these records could well become a major source of information. Much of the testimony is revealing and some of it is fascinating to anyone curious as to how people try to evaluate institutions of higher education and what accreditation means or doesn't mean. But that is a long story in itself. Here I must be content to record the court's decision.

In July, 1969 the United States District Judge, John Lewis Smith, Jr., rendered an opinion that was a complete victory for the college. He fully sustained the plaintiff on both the antitrust count and the constitutional count. The court found that the college in particular, and higher education in general, were indeed engaged in trade and commerce in which the element of competition is often strong; that Middle States by itself and Middle States together with the other regionals were both "combinations" in unreasonable restraint of trade; that they were performing governmental functions to such an extent as to require them to observe constitutional restraints; and that their policy of excluding proprietary institutions was "arbitrary, unreasonable, and contrary to the public interest." The court denied a request from Middle States to suspend the injunction pending an appeal of the decision to a higher court, and ordered Middle States to visit and evaluate the college and to accredit it if the college met Middle States' normal standards apart from the proprietary exclusion.

The trial proved to be a revealing, if not very reassuring, examination of the regional associations; and the decision, if it is upheld on appeal, will have important effects on higher education and quite possibly on the lower schools as well. It will mean that an important precedent is established which says that the regional associations are not beyond the law's reach. It may also mean that the way is open for litigation in the future on such murky but fundamental questions as the adequacy of the standards and criteria themselves employed by the regionals. Moreover, the decision lends great support to the idea that competition is a good thing in education, that competition should be free so that all kinds of institutions can operate in the market place on equal terms, and that American education should preserve as many options and alternatives as possible.

Did Parsons Deserve to Be Disaccredited?

This question is not quite the same as this one: "Was NCA justified in disaccrediting Parsons?" And neither question is quite the same as this one: "Did Parsons receive justice from the court?" To the last question I would answer yes. The court narrowed the issues to those it felt competent to rule on and made only one major determination—that Parsons had been accorded due process within the established procedures of NCA. It did not rule on the wisdom of those procedures, much less on the wisdom of NCA's standards or of the way it conducts the general business of evaluating institutions. Those procedures and standards, however, are central to the problem of whether Parsons received justice at the hands of NCA.

On the question of whether Parsons deserved disaccreditation, I would answer with a strongly qualified yes; but on the question of whether Parsons deserved to be disaccredited in the way NCA did it, I would answer with a strongly qualified no. Those answers are not, I hope, mere hairsplitting or pettifoggery. The difference in the answers goes to the heart of regional accreditation and to the matter of trying to reform it.

When I say that Parsons deserved to be disaccredited, I mean that any institution following the policies and practices that Parsons followed for most of Roberts's administration ought to be censured and restrained in the public interest until it corrects the problems. I believe, that is, that Parsons did misrepresent itself to the degree, did engage in unethical practices sufficiently serious, and did fail so often to come through on promises to correct problems repeatedly called to its attention, that decisive action to protect the public was needed. That action, however, need not have been disaccreditation with the enormous damage it does to students and to many other innocent people. The same end could have been achieved, and I believe should have been, by earlier, more consistent, and more informed action from NCA.

But such action was probably not in the cards and dis-accreditation therefore probably unavoidable. For the basic fact about regional accreditation is that it is normally a rather quiet, clubby, pedestrian enterprise that involves a lot of log-rolling, not to say a kind of academic incest in which repre-sentatives of the member institutions visit one another's schools, sit alternately on various committees, and alternately make decisions about one another's schools. It is all an un-eventful and not very lively enterprise that is not well equipped to handle unprecedented situations.

However, the customary blandness of the regional associa-tions does not mean that they have little power. Quite the contrary. No institution can afford to ignore or opt out of them. Although they call themselves voluntary associations, the court in the Majorie Webster case found that they re-semble monopolies. They exercise a great deal of influence, beneficial or baleful depending on one's bias, over the direc-tion of higher education. Unfortunately, they do not attract many scholars or men of real distinction, either on visiting teams or in other capacities. They seem to have an appeal for educational administrators, especially presidents of small col-leges and people who call themselves "professional educators" (those who specialize in the study of education itself).

Like most educational bureaucracies, the regionals are noted more for caution than courage, more for inertia than imagina-tion. They are all but unknown to the general public except when something like the Parsons problem comes along, at which time the public assumes that anything called a profes-sional accrediting agency must have God on its side. The fact is that the Parsons incident demonstrates, and not for the first time, a number of serious deficiencies within the regional accrediting agencies that ought to be corrected. Let's see what a few of them were and how they affected Parsons.

Inadequate Reports and Dubious Standards. The validity and effectiveness of the criteria used by the regionals to evaluate institutions are important issues. In years past the regionals relied, and some still do, mostly on quantitative measurements such as expenditure per student and the number of books in the library. But they claim to have shifted some years ago to more qualitative and less artificial standards in response to criticism from the institutions themselves. In fact visiting teams now use a highly imprecise mixture of both. The regionals now tell their member institutions that they will be evaluated only on how well the institutions are doing whatever job it is they have defined for themselves. But it rarely works out that way, for institutions are forever being compared by visiting teams not only with the somewhat mystical standards of the individual examiners but with some kind of dimly perceived national standard. From reliance on one system that was too mechanical, the regionals have now moved to one that is too vague and subjective.

The NCA reports on Parsons are a classic study in the unreliability of visiting team reports. They are an eloquent demonstration of the fact that three or four people cannot spend two or three days at a strange institution the size of Parsons and accurately evaluate it. To begin with, the bevy of NCA examiners who visited Parsons during Roberts's administration had no way of assessing how well Parsons was doing the job it had set out to do, for the job was a new one for which there were no agreed-upon standards of success. NCA could determine well enough that Parsons was not doing everything it claimed to be doing, but that is not the same problem as determining whether Parsons was successful as an open-door and a second-chance college.

The reports on Parsons are full of impressionistic comments, both negative and positive, from the examiners, and of unverified assumptions about the way a college should be run. Ironically, Parsons may have lost its accreditation precisely because NCA no longer based its assessments solely on specific, quantified standards—which Roberts would have bent over backwards to meet—but instead based them on a set of general and rather elusive standards in which the personal feelings and predilections of the examiners had to play a major part—which Roberts could scarcely know how to anticipate or meet.

If one compares the 1963 report on Parsons, which put the college on probation, with the 1964 report, which took it off probation, one could ask for no better illustration of the dangers and dubieties of the present method of evaluating institutions. The 1963 report was, I believe, more accurate than that in 1964 but was also filled with vitriolic judgments that should have called into question the whole report. Unfortunately I cannot quote from the report for the reasons already cited, but I would submit that no self-respecting accrediting agency ought to be willing to take a negative action so serious as putting an institution on probation on the basis of such a document as the 1963 report.

As it turned out, that report, for all its failings, was a better overall analysis than the one that followed it, but NCA could certainly not have known that at the time, and Parsons would have every right to feel suspicious of an accrediting group that would put it on public probation on the strength of such an abusive and tendentious report. Moreover, both the 1963 and 1964 reports were wrong on important points of fact and interpretation.

The 1967 report, which was the announced basis of disaccreditation, was even less accurate though also less impassioned than that in 1963. First, the 1967 report was simply wrong on a fairly large number of matters, especially in regard to Parsons's finances which, when correctly understood, were stronger in 1967 than they had ever been in the past, when they were considered one of Parsons's virtues by NCA. Both the college and its auditors, Price Waterhouse and Company, wrote rebuttals to this report, pointing out the substantial

errors; as also did the college's financial manager in an affi-
davit used in the Parsons lawsuit and a large number of
faculty members who also signed affidavits regarding one or
another facet of the 1967 NCA visit and report. But all that,
of course, was too late to prevent the damage that was done
by NCA's announcement of disaccreditation.

John O. Hall, a man who has followed Parsons closely and
is now in charge of institutional research at the University
of Pittsburgh, commented to me on the 1967 report this way:

> I think the 1967 report was very poor. It was very super-
> ficial and erroneous in many respects; it was not a balanced
> report at all. I don't think it was because the visiting team
> was prejudiced or out to get Parsons. I think they had the
> same difficulties of any accrediting job when the time is
> limited. . . . [but] if you're going to be as casual and blasé
> about accreditation as this report was, NCA can really do
> some damage. The result of this is that there will be a
> great number of colleges in the NCA area that will hesitate
> to experiment.

I agree with that comment but would add that the 1967 report
was on the whole favorable to Parsons and in fact recommended that the accreditation of the college be continued.
The mischief lay in the weight given the negative aspects of
this imperfect report by NCA.

That changes need to be made in the assessment techniques
of the regionals, and even more perhaps in how they use the
reports they get, was recognized even by William K. Selden,
then head of the National Commission of Accrediting (an
agency that in effect accredits accrediting agencies) and who
was no opponent of regional accrediting, when he wrote:

> We still have not learned how to judge the real quality of a
> college or university. Even though the regional associations

now place much less reliance on specific, detailed, quantitative measurements, they continue to confront institutions with prodigious criteria and voluminous questionnaires, few of which have been verified as to their reliability in distinguishing an excellent college or an outstanding university. Reliance on empirical judgment, as presently demanded, places almost unlimited responsibility on the corps of visiting evaluators and the members of the commissions in each regional association who are charged with the obligation of making not only constructive, dynamic, and far-seeing suggestions but consistent, unbiased, and sound decisions.

Fortunately for all higher education many individuals are convinced that the time is arriving for a new analysis of accrediting—this time on a broad cooperative basis. However, if the regional associations do not squarely face the question of the soundness of their methods and the validity of their criteria, other forces will develop and challenge the authority of the colleges and universities to evaluate themselves through their own accrediting organizations.[2]

Perhaps the greatest single failing of the regionals has been the lack of good research on their own standards and procedures. As far as I know, they have never done such a simple thing as, for example, sending two different but matched visiting teams to the same school and comparing their reports. Only one attempt, to my knowledge, has been made even to compare analytically the visiting team reports that have already been done and are in the files. This was a study of eighty-seven reports in the NCA files a few years ago which demonstrated certain problems that are still a long way from solution. The study found that only about 14 per cent of the "statements" made in these reports were "facts, reports, citations, or questions." The other 86 per cent were "judgmental statements" based on observation and undocumented conclusions. The study further corroborates the commonly known fact that examiners rarely try to look at what comes *out* of an institution in the way of graduates but only at what goes *into* the program in the way of money, curricula, organization, and so forth, and that even these matters are left pretty much to the personal judgment of the examiners:

> The lack of application of external norms on salaries, [teaching] load, library holdings, and the like is also a strength and a weakness. On the one hand, it reflects the disposition of the examiners to appraise each institution on its own terms rather than to judge it on the basis of possibly irrelevant criteria. On the other hand, it reflects the lack of acceptable norms in sufficient detail for application to widely differing institutions, and this lack of objective data forces examiners to make general and undocumented judgments.[3]

Accreditation is a big subject, one we cannot treat fully here. The relevant point is simple: the methods used by the regionals to evaluate institutions are not reliable enough for anyone to be able to say what it means to be a "fully accredited" institution or why an accredited institution is better than an unaccredited one. Lacking such reliability, I believe it is incumbent on these agencies to build into their procedures some safeguards against unjustly punitive or unreasonably biased decisions. If such machinery had existed within NCA, Parsons might have been severely censured and forced to reform, as it should have been, but might have been spared the trauma of disaccreditation.

A Penchant for Conformity. Higher education in the United States, in spite of all that is said to the contrary, is notable for its lack of experimentation. Deviation from conventional wisdom is rare. The reasons for this inertia are many, but regional accreditation is a major one, and Parsons demonstrates the point. The NCA reports on Parsons make it clear that NCA was not content to judge the institution, as it claimed, on the institution's own terms. The NCA reports frequently compare Parsons with other schools and complain about Parsons's departures from "accepted practices" in education. Examiners expected Parsons to produce data that conformed to the orthodox two-semester academic year; they expected it to have a student-teacher ratio comparable to the majority of institutions; they expected it to maintain faculty teaching loads in line with other institutions. They apparently could not adjust to the fact that Parsons was trying to take some new paths that might not lend themselves neatly to the usual methods of assessment or to comparison with orthodox institutions.

Nels F. S. Ferre, distinguished scholar in residence at Parsons, comments that

> The reason NCA took the action it did was because of all the small colleges in Iowa that felt threatened by Parsons— I couldn't believe some of the things these colleges said out of sheer fear and prejudice. I think the NCA would like Parsons to become just one of the little colleges in Iowa, innocent of innovation.

Another senior professor and supporter of Roberts, Kenneth W. Perry (the college's most highly paid professor in the Roberts era), comments:

> Roberts created a lot of his own problems, but his real sin in the NCA was rocking the boat. They don't want you to be creative. If you're creative, they'll kill you like they did Parsons.

While I doubt that the regional associations are quite that inflexible or that they subject every new idea to the guillotine with conscious premeditation, their whole operation is geared to the maintenance of the status quo, not to the sympathetic appraisal of new ideas, much less to the stimulation of them. One or another of the reports on Parsons exhibits not only overt criticism of Parsons's departures from orthodoxy but covert prejudices against, for example, the high salaries of the faculty, or the stipulated curriculum of the first two years, or other aspects of the Parsons Plan that the examiners, perhaps subconsciously, found personally offensive.

To reinforce the pressures for conformity exercised by visiting teams, NCA maintains a roster of trained consultants to serve its member institutions or institutions that want to qualify for membership. Not only does NCA *offer* the services of such consultants, it *requires* many institutions, including Parsons, to take and pay for such consultants if they want to be accredited. NCA talks a lot about respecting institutional autonomy but sees no inconsistency in forcing its own consultants on some of its schools and forcing them to pay not only the consultation fee and expenses but an overhead rate to NCA itself. NCA in some years has earned about as much money from this activity as it has from membership dues. Such a coercive policy inevitably exerts pressure on colleges to conform to what NCA and its consultants have decided is the "right" way of running institutions of higher education. Thus the institutions that have the most trouble with NCA are those that doubt there is a "right" way and want to try something new.

Nor is there only one "right" way even among the regionals. It depends on which of the six jurisdictions a college is in, for there is no necessary comparability among the six regional associations; what is accreditable, or disaccreditable, in one may not be so in another. Their standards and certainly their internal procedures differ. "It is," as one Parsons professor remarked, "a sort of floating crap game." One of the interesting questions about Parsons is what would have happened to it in other regions. The answer can only be guesswork, obviously, but my own guess is that Parsons would have been handled differently in at least four of the other five regions and might never have come to the sad pass in any of them that it did in NCA's territory. In short, what is thought of as justice in Chicago might well be injustice in Baltimore or Los Angeles.

Since the federal government began to inject large funds into higher education, the regionals have been trying to cope with the lack of comparability among themselves. They have created an organization called the Federation of Regional Accrediting Commissions of Higher Education (FRACHE), though the primary motivation may have been less a concern for their differing standards as a concern to ward off the threat of national or governmental accreditation. Whether FRACHE will be able to bring any sort of standardization into regional accrediting remains to be seen. Even if it does, that kind of committee-created standardization might be worse, and more dedicated to orthodoxy and conformity, than the six regionals now are. It is hard to see how the regionals can be made less rigid unless the member institutions themselves are concerned enough about the present system to demand changes.

Secrecy and Capricious Procedures. For a tax-exempt educational organization devoted to the improvement of colleges and universities and supposedly to the protection of the public, NCA operates behind an inappropriate mask of secrecy. Whatever the main purpose of this secrecy, it nicely shields NCA from inconvenience and criticism. In view of the power that has accrued to the regional accrediting bodies, especially their taking on of governmental responsibilities, they should be required, I believe, to operate more in the open than they do.

There is, for instance, no very persuasive reason why the

reports of visiting teams should not be public documents and very good reasons why they should be. If the regionals have any faith in their standards and criteria, they should make the publication of reports a policy and a condition of membership. The regionals can no doubt think of a good many reasons why public disclosure would not be a sound policy, and it indeed might be an embarrassment to some educational administrators; but the benefits would far outweigh the disadvantages. One of the greatest benefits would be to insure the preparation of more careful and accurate reports.

Nor is there any reason why those groups within NCA and the other regionals charged with making the basic decisions about institutions should not operate in the public arena. The executive board, for example, which is the group that finally decides the fate of institutions within NCA, should conduct its deliberations in a goldfish bowl. That would be an inconvenience on some occasions but both the institutions and the public would be served by such a procedure, which would be a safeguard against capricious or biased decisions. As it now is, the executive board operates in a secrecy so complete that it does not even record its deliberations in minutes; only its decisions.

One of the most interesting exhibits of the Parsons lawsuit was a document that purported to be the minutes of the executive board meeting at which the decision to disaccredit Parsons was made. The minutes that record the executive board decision are exactly seven lines long. On the witness stand, Norman Burns, NCA's executive secretary, was asked about these records:

Question: Dr. Burns, this single sheet of paper, Plaintiff's Exhibit 17, represents the only minutes of both the meeting of the Executive Board on April 4th and the meeting of the Commission on April 5th, is that true?
Answer: Yes, I think that can be stated that way.

Nor were there any minutes of the so-called committee by type, which is a body that reviews, according to the "type" of institutions involved, the visiting team reports and makes recommendations to the executive board about what should be done with a given institution. Thus Parsons, far from having a transcript of what was said about it, or even steno-graphic notes or reasonable minutes, or even a record of who voted for what from either of the two bodies within NCA that determined its fate, has two single sheets of paper that cryptically record decisions and recommendations—and has those only by virtue of having taken NCA to court. It would seem reasonable to expect an educational accrediting organ-ization that claims to operate in the public interest to conduct its affairs in a different fashion from this.

At the very least, the regionals should have some well-defined safety procedures that they must follow before taking negative action against a member institution. On July 15, 1968 I made the following suggestion in a letter to Mr. Burns of NCA:

Let me reiterate my suggestion about public disclosure in cases of disaccreditation. What I suggest is simply this: In all cases where a regional accrediting body . . . dis-accredits an institution, it should make public the visiting team reports and other related documents. It might pos-sibly do so as well in cases of probation or in taking other action that is seriously damaging to the institution involved. Such public disclosure could easily be made a condition of membership in North Central or any other body.

The advantages seem to me great and the disadvantages very small. The requirement of full public disclosure would surely operate as a powerful incentive to an institution to *avoid* probation or disaccreditation in the first place. It would also be some assurance against prejudice, real or imagined, on the part of the accreditors. And it would avoid speculative, malicious, or ill-informed articles or books based, as has been and will continue to be the case with Parsons, on incomplete or distorted information. Finally, the public interest would be served by making available to parents, and laymen in general, information about the specific weaknesses of the institution involved.

As to the disadvantages, the institution would already have been severely damaged by the action taken, and moreover would presumably owe it to the public to have its deficiencies revealed.

I can't help feeling that *all* parties involved in the Parsons case would have been better off if this kind of public disclosure had been made. Of course it is conceivable that, had public disclosure been a condition of membership in North Central, Parsons would never have reached the point where deleterious action would have been taken.

Although I did not receive an answer to this proposal, I still feel that the regionals in general and NCA in particular ought to examine the question of whether their function as guardians of the public, and in particular their function as quasi-governmental and secondary licensing authorities, ought not to dictate an operation that is less shrouded in secrecy. Although the regionals powerfully affect the public, they do not seem in any way answerable to the public.

In addition to the problem of NCA's secrecy, Parsons might justly feel aggrieved by what can only be called NCA's capricious procedures. The first example was NCA's reaction to The Dissident Report. Even though I believe, as I have said, that the major charges brought by the dissidents were true and that they needed to be made, there was a vaguely conspiratorial air about their conferring quietly in advance with NCA. An accrediting agency should rely on its own resources and not on informers to keep abreast of its institutions, and in any case should not be dealing with an institution behind the back of the president, no matter how disenchanted it may be with him.

More serious than that were the irregularities in the way NCA conducted the 1963 visit and reached its decision to put the college on probation. The principal irregularity was in putting the college on "public" probation—that is, by publicly circulating an announcement of its action. Before 1963 NCA put offending institutions on what was called simply "probation" without a public statement, but it chose to publicize the probation in this case "to offset," as Norman Burns told a Parsons official, "these false claims [of the college] and to inform other institutions that the NCA would not condone this kind of practice."

I have no quarrel with public probation and indeed think it advisable provided the decision is arrived at in a way that is open to public scrutiny and provided that it is not an *ex post facto* procedure—as it was with Parsons. The possibility that a school's probation will be given special publicity in certain cases should be clearly spelled out in the conditions of membership, or NCA should not have pulled it out of the hat especially for Parsons. Even if it were an established rather than an ad hoc procedure, NCA ought to have reached its decision in a more equitable fashion than it did and on the basis of a more balanced and less impassioned report.

Then in 1966 with the appearance of the *Life* article on Parsons, NCA resumed its special handling of the college. I doubt that there has ever been another accreditation visit made to a college on the basis of an article in a popular magazine. Nor should there have been this time. Indeed if that is now to be the policy of NCA, I can think of at least a dozen major institutions in NCA's territory that are being or have very recently been seriously compromised by student dissidents, the quality of the instructional program significantly damaged, and a great deal of bad publicity created. I wonder what NCA is doing about them. Is it sending visiting teams to the University of Chicago, Wisconsin, Michigan? John Diekhoff, an NCA consultant to Parsons at the time of the *Life* article, wrote a heated letter to Burns after NCA's decision to send a team to the college, as follows:

> The decision of the NCA Board to send a review team to Parsons College this Fall seems to me unfair to Parsons College. The report of the team that went to Parsons in December 1964 recommended a regular review visit "three or four years from now," which would be not earlier than December, 1967. And the Association [NCA] specified the employment of a consultant—me, as it happens—to work with Parsons during the period between visits. I have been to Parsons only twice. The Executive Committee had access only to the report on my first visit. If there are advantages to a college in working with a North Central consultant, Parsons can hardly have had the benefit of them—but now must prepare for and submit to a review visit on very short notice.
>
> If the Board had asked my advice before taking action, I would certainly have advised against the action taken. Moreover, I think I should have been asked.
>
> If the North Central Association undertakes unscheduled review visits to every college subjected to unfavorable publicity, it will be a very busy association indeed. If it lets irresponsible journalists shape its policies or direct its relationships with its member institutions, it shares their irresponsibility. And if it ignores its consultants in dealing with its member colleges, it will soon run out of consultants.[4]

NCA also departed from a number of its announced policies in the way it sent the 1967 team to Parsons. Having received the team's report with its heavy emphasis on Parsons's finances, some of it ill-informed, NCA then disaccredited the institution. One strongly suspects that NCA does not worry so much about the finances of its other member institutions, for if it did, many of them that are in far worse shape than Parsons was would presumably have to be disaccredited. Again, Parsons might justly complain of ad hoc procedures.

More unusual still was the fact that both the visiting team and the type committee recommended to the NCA executive board that Parsons's accreditation be continued. The executive board vetoed the recommendations of both previous reviewing bodies. "NCA seems to have put," says Irwin Lubbers, a former NCA president, "more faith in journalists than in their own examiners." A total of thirteen people, all of whom knew more about the college than the executive board and four of whom had recently spent several days on the campus, were vetoed by a group of six people, only one of whom had ever been to the college and who had made that visit four years earlier.

Of the six members of the executive board voting for disaccreditation, two were not present for the full discussion but voted afterwards by telephone. One cannot be sure of precedents in view of NCA's secrecy, but I would be astonished if any other college in NCA history has been disaccredited in this fashion and in the face of contrary recommendations from both the visiting team and the type committee. Again the only reason that Parsons ever discovered how its fate was settled by six men, three of whom had also been involved in the 1963 probation, two of whom were not even present for the full deliberations, was by taking NCA to court and getting the documents on the record.

NCA did not break its bylaws by so acting, but the manner in which the executive board disaccredited Parsons does little to reinforce one's faith in the dispassionate justice of the organization. (The executive board, by the way, did the same thing in 1968 with still another visiting team's report that recommended reaccreditation for the college.) Nor is it at all clear why the executive board is more competent to make the final determination on a school than the people who actually visit the school, or more competent than the type committee which reviews the documents and listens to oral presentations from both the visiting team and the school involved. The same people, after all, can be found serving on all three groups at various times. Imperfect as visiting team reports might be, it seems obvious that the authors of them have a better knowledge of the institution than people who have never set foot on the campus. One would think the executive board might be the least competent of the three groups!

Not content with this history of special treatment of Parsons, NCA then issued a "public statement" of disaccreditation, something that it had never done with an institution before, and made it public before it had notified Parsons itself of the disaccreditation. Burns said to me that this action was taken "for the sake of other institutions rather than the general public," but he agrees that the basic function of NCA is "to protect the public."

Again, I have no quarrel with such a public statement in cases of disaccreditation and think there is much to be said for it. What troubles me are all of the ad hoc and special procedures engaged in by NCA to deal with its Parsons problem. Moreover, NCA as a member of the Federation of Regional Accrediting Commissions of Higher Education clearly violated FRACHE's "Code of Good Practice," which says in part that the members of FRACHE agree "to revoke accreditation only after advance notice has been given to the president of an institution that such action is contemplated, and the reasons therefor, sufficient to permit timely rejoinder." The code also says that the members of FRACHE agree to such matters as these:

> to evaluate or visit an institution or program of study only on the express invitation of the president or, when the action

is initiated by the organization with respect to an institution already accredited by the organization, with the specific authorization of the president of the institution or his officially designated representative . . .

to use relevant qualitative and quantitative information in its evaluation process . . .

to conduct any evaluation visit to an institution by experienced and qualified examiners *under conditions that assure impartial and objective judgment* [my italics] . . .

to provide adequate opportunity for inclusion of students in the interviewing process during accrediting visits [something none of the NCA reports on Parsons did] . . .

to refrain from conditioning accreditation upon payment of fees for purposes other than membership dues or actual evaluation costs . . .

Taking it all into consideration, one has a very difficult time in persuading oneself that Parsons had the benefit of equal application of the accrediting laws. The bitterness of many Parsons people about NCA is entirely understandable. Unfortunately they are in no position to express that bitterness right now when they are trying desperately to get back into the club.

What, then, *should* NCA have done about Parsons College? For the fact remains that Parsons did deserve to be censured and should indeed have been compelled to reform in order to remain in good standing in NCA. First, NCA should have moved in on Parsons before 1963 and thereby avoided the erratic actions NCA took later on. There were plenty of early warnings. As we saw in Chapter 6, lots of people who were in a position to know what was happening at the college, especially people in the church, were pressing for action even in 1959 and 1960. There is reason to believe that NCA too, and the National Council for Accreditation of Teacher Education, knew what was going on at Parsons, but still NCA did not act. Certainly enough was known by 1961 to warrant a full NCA investigation. At that point NCA could have accomplished a great deal by launching such an investigation and making it clear to Roberts that real changes would have to be made, or if necessary of taking up matters directly with the board of trustees. But NCA instead sat fretfully on its hands.

Failing action in 1961 or 1962, NCA should not have removed Parsons from probation in 1965. Not enough improvement had been made in the preceding year and a half to justify this removal. And failing that, NCA should have gone directly to the trustees in 1966 or 1967 and made clear to them that changes could no longer be delayed. And failing even that, NCA should certainly have gone about the final act in a more equitable way.

Perhaps most of all, NCA should have organized more thorough examinations of the college when it became clear that it could not or should not base such serious decisions as probation or disaccreditation on the reports it had in hand. As a matter of future policy, NCA ought to require that a much more comprehensive evaluation than Parsons ever received be made of an institution before damaging action is taken against a member college. It most certainly should do so when its executive board proposes to veto the recommendations of the people who actually visited the institution, not to say the recommendations of the committee by type as well. That kind of split opinion should automatically call for a return to the institution and a more thorough investigation before final action is taken.

In brief, NCA with a bit more skill could have cured its problem with Parsons at a dozen different points in time short of disaccreditation and could thereby have avoided serious injury to many students, parents, to not a few members of the Parsons staff, and, most importantly, to what might have been a valuable experiment in higher education. But NCA failed to meet the challenge. Instead it vacillated at first, then took a variety of insensitive, obtuse, or capricious actions that ended in overkill. Those who praise NCA's action ought to ask themselves whether it does not in actuality represent a defeat instead of a victory for the accrediting process. *L'affaire Parsons* will not go down as one of the nobler chapters in NCA history, but it says a lot about regional accreditation in the United States. Who indeed, as Juvenal asked, "will stand guard over the guards themselves?"

N O T E S

[1] *Journal of Higher Education* (November, 1959), p. 430.

[2] William K. Selden, *Accreditation: A Struggle Over Standards in Higher Education* (New York: Harper, 1960), pp. 43–44.

[3] Paul Dressel, "Some Observations on NCA Examiners Reports," *NCA Quarterly* (Fall, 1967), p. 216.

[4] Plaintiff Exhibit 9 from the Parsons lawsuit.

Epilogue

The middle sort of historians, of which the most part are, spoil all; they will chew our meat for us.

—MONTAIGNE

"Tut, tut, child," said the Duchess. "Everything's got a moral if only you can find it."

—LEWIS CARROLL

. . . if all liberal colleges had the same aim, and if they were serious in pursuit of it, the differences among them would become, for a change, really interesting.

—MARK VAN DOREN

Not many educators feel "the sensuous joy of magnanimity," as Turgenev described it, when they contemplate the Parsons record. Instead too many educators apply a double standard, one to Parsons and another to the rest of the world of higher education. That Parsons has much to answer for is abundantly clear to readers who have come this far with me, but what is not clear is why more should have been expected of Parsons than of other colleges and universities. The future, if any, of the Parsons Plan has much to do with the attitude of American educators in general. Perhaps their final judgment about the college should be made in the light of the fact that most of the errors and weaknesses of which Parsons was guilty from 1955 to 1967 can be found today in more institutions in good standing than Parsons's critics would care to admit.

I can think, for instance, of an institution that achieved full accreditation from NCA within the last few years that has about the same high ratio of students to faculty as Parsons had; that has very large lecture courses but no preceptors or tutors; that offers very little personal contact between the teachers and the taught; that has a tightly restricted curriculum; that has salaries far below those of Parsons; and that makes a handsome profit in the same sense that Parsons did. Nobody is giving it any difficulty, much less threatening to disaccredit it.

I can think of many colleges whose general financial situation is much more grim than that of Parsons ever was. I can think of institutions with strong-man presidents who have no very great regard for faculty rights and privileges. I can think of institutions that are glad to take in every student they can get, including rejects from Parsons. I can think of some that charge every bit of tuition they think the market will bear. I can think of a great many with mickey-mouse courses in profusion and with faculties infinitely weaker than that of Parsons. And I can think of some whose advertising and promotional activities are less energetic and misleading but are a long way from the whole truth.

Nor were Parsons's other sins unique. Grade manipulation, for example, especially for athletic purposes, is hardly a new phenomenon in American education. Recruiters who distort the truth were not invented by Parsons. Acrimonious administrators, dubious deans, and pusillanimous professors are nothing new under the sun—as has been demonstrated far more compellingly in recent years at the very best American institutions than it was at Parsons.

As for greed, "the universities," as Robert Maynard Hutchins recently commented, "have demonstrated their willingness to do almost anything for money." And their administrators and faculties are richly entangled, as James Ridgeway has shown,[1] with the federal government in general and the Department of Defense in particular, and with corporate and industrial America—a relationship in which academics frequently trade on the name of their home institutions for private gain. The universities themselves, far from engaging in full disclosure as might be expected of institutions that spend so much public money, frequently decline to produce financial reports and auditors' opinions for public distribution. Some of our penurious colleges, for their part, also behave in ways that are less than admirable, as described by Paul Woodring:

> In their efforts to survive, the weaker colleges have made questionable claims and have resorted to futile tactics. Some have insisted that educational quality is unrelated to faculty salaries. Many have claimed too much for the hallowed tradition, the intimate environment, and the low student-teacher ratio. Some, while boasting of their freedom from political control, have abjectly accepted the equally stultifying controls of provincialism and parochialism. While condemning state colleges as godless they have themselves substituted piety for learning. Some, while retaining the name of liberal arts colleges, have transformed themselves into low-grade vocational schools. In an effort to attract students, some have expanded their lists of course offerings without expanding their faculties or facilities.[2]

None of this in any way excuses the abuses and disabilities of Parsons that I have detailed in previous chapters; that much I trust is clear. I want only to suggest that the air of moral superiority taken so often by other educators towards Parsons may be less appropriate than an honest admission that Parsons's offenses, while a shade darker and more tenacious than those of other colleges, are not much different in kind. Avoiding a double standard may not be easy, but it is obviously necessary if one's ultimate verdict on Parsons is to be a fair one.

The Satellite Colleges

Whatever future the Parsons Plan has may ride with the so-called satellite or sister colleges that Roberts coached into being during the later years of his administration. Six of them were created by small midwestern communities as a result of Roberts's pep talks to chambers of commerce and other groups who were understandably taken with the idea of a profit-making college in town. The six were:

Charles City College—Charles City, Iowa
College of Artesia—Artesia, New Mexico
Hiram Scott College—Scottsbluff, Nebraska
John J. Pershing College—Beatrice, Nebraska
Lea College—Albert Lea, Minnesota
Midwestern College—Denison, Iowa

Under Roberts's guidance, other communities, such as Council Bluffs, Iowa, also developed plans for "self-amortizing" colleges but did not bring them to fruition. Roberts drew up detailed financial and organizational proposals for still other colleges as far away as Riverside, California, but they too failed for various reasons to materialize. The idea of Parsons's reproducing itself seems to have started in the early 1960's when Roberts came close to buying a campus at Carthage, Illinois that had been left vacant when the institution that had previously occupied it moved to a new location. Roberts got a grant from the Ford Foundation to make a feasibility study of buying Carthage but abandoned the idea for several reasons, including the recommendations of his consultants that Parsons first recover its full accreditation (it was then on probation) and tone down its "commercial" public relations campaign.

Roberts was convinced that a limitless market for higher education existed in the United States and that students could be recruited in quantity for the indefinite future. He may have been right, but he was wrong in thinking that such students could be lured to private open-door, low-prestige colleges in sufficient numbers to finance a string of Parsonses across the country.

The six satellites that were established had serious troubles from the beginning. Charles City College went bankrupt in 1968 at the end of its first year of operation, and most of the others face a very uncertain future. Only one of the six, Hiram Scott College, seems to be doing well financially and to show good prospects. It was the only one by 1969 to have been given the status of Recognized Candidate for Accreditation by NCA, although two others had been given Correspondent status, which is the minimum available. Hiram Scott was also the only one with an enrollment of over one thousand students. Of the remaining four (apart, that is, from Hiram Scott and Charles City), Lea College probably has the best chance of survival and may well become the best in academic and general quality. The others have suffered from severe administrative problems, from high turnover in both faculty and administration, from low enrollments, from internal strife, and from uncertain community support and other difficulties.

Because these colleges were so closely identified with Parsons, they have all been caught in the backwash of Parsons's disaccreditation and negative publicity. None of the offshoot colleges now maintains any formal ties with Parsons, although several still owe the college money for salaries, supplies, and services that had originally been advanced by Parsons to get the colleges started. All of them are now anxious to disassociate themselves from their origins and to gain recognition from NCA.

The offshoot colleges follow the main ideas of the Parsons

Plan. They carry on the same kind of aggressive recruiting of students in the northeastern states as did Parsons, and they take in a high percentage of marginal and drop-out students. Most of them offer full-scale summer study, not only because of financial necessity but also because remedial or "early start" summer students do not have to be counted into such institutional measures as average College Board scores (which are usually calculated on the basis of the regular fall entering class). These colleges also have to struggle, as did Parsons in the nature of things, with an intellectually apathetic student body in which the eastern element often offends the local community and in which drugs, liquor, and vandalism are common problems, as indeed they are on other campuses.

None of these colleges has taken the Parsons Plan unaltered, and no two of them are exactly alike. "I learned at Parsons what not to do," says the dean of one of them, which in a sense is true of all of them. Some have followed the Parsons team teaching system but with greater attention to its weaknesses as revealed at Parsons. Some have profited from Parsons's mistake of creating three distinct classes of teachers and have adopted a different approach. All have a restricted curriculum of the Parsons type, although in differing degrees. All have tried to get well-qualified faculty members at competitive salaries, but none has tried to match the Parsons pay scale. All have put a major emphasis on teaching and on close student-faculty relationships, though the practice is not equal to the theory.

In short these offshoot colleges—it is no longer fair to call them satellites, for they are wholly on their own now—are all roughly within the Parsons formula with its major strengths and some of its weaknesses. But they also have the freedom to test the Parsons Plan in a way that Parsons itself never could, and to change it on the basis of experience. Unfortunately they are so busy right now fighting for existence that significant experimentation will probably not be possible for a while. If one or two of them can overcome their financial problems, escape "the mark of Cain" that clings rather stubbornly to them, and get themselves fully accredited, they may well become interesting centers of experimentation. If the essence of the Parsons Plan is to be applied anywhere with success, it presumably will have the best chance at whichever of these colleges is able to stay in business.

Parsons after Roberts

If anyone doubted the importance of accreditation, Parsons's experience upon the loss of its accreditation ought to eliminate that doubt. Parsons immediately lost over half its students, not to mention losing the growth in enrollment that it had been expecting in the fall of 1967; and the decline continued for some time, moving Parsons from a college of 5,000 students to one of 1,500 in the spring of 1969. Parsons students lost certain government benefits as well as the easy transfer of credits to other institutions and to graduate schools. The quality of the student body also declined, after starting to rise in the last couple of years of Roberts's regime. The ability of Parsons's recruiters to gain admittance to high schools also declined. Charles F. Barnett, head of the Parsons admissions office, comments that after the disaccreditation, "Some high schools would not let us in the door. Some let us in to give us hell. And some sympathized but were helpless."

A crash program of retrenchment had to be undertaken. Parsons's agreements with the Connecticut insurance companies that held the lion's share of the college's long-term debts required the college to maintain its accreditation or to be in default. But cooperation and assistance, rather than foreclosure were clearly indicated by Parsons's creditors if they hoped to recover their investments. Parsons renegotiated a total of $14 million in debts. It hammered out a plan that included a two-year moratorium on interest payments and that thereafter would allow the college to pay off about $1 million in debt each year with an enrollment of 2,000 students. The enrollment could fall as low as 1,500 for a time and still not bankrupt the college. Parsons even managed to float additional emergency loans on the strength of its financial record and its determination to achieve economies that had never been possible under Roberts.

The faculty of course took a drubbing. Some people resigned, some were put on leave that will probably turn out to be permanent, and a number were in effect fired. From a total teaching force of 255 at the time of disaccreditation, Parsons went down to 80 the following fall. In the top ranks, over half the full professors left; and in the bottom ranks, practically all the tutors left. The rank of preceptor was abolished, and those preceptors who remained were elevated to the rank of instructor, thus eliminating the controversial and ambiguous rankings that went with the Parsons system of team teaching. The salaries of those people who remained at Parsons were not as badly cut as one might imagine and today still match the salaries of very good colleges and universities.

There was general administrative turmoil for a while aggravated by a severe outbreak of campus politicking. One insider was appointed acting president to succeed Roberts but soon returned to his old faculty position, whereupon another insider was appointed acting president, but he too left the job. Finally another insider was made full president, thus giving Parsons the experience of four presidents in two years, a feat that some other institutions may be matching before the great student rebellion of the late 1960's has run its course. Old Roberts hands were gradually eased out of the college as the new administration shaped up.

Everybody, of course, suffered from the all-but-fatal dose of bad publicity that accompanied the disaccreditation. Other colleges became even more wary of Parsons than they already were. Students wanting to transfer from Parsons to other institutions were sometimes told that no credit whatever would be given for work they had done and that they would have to start again as freshmen if they wanted to move. One student, so the story goes, had his transfer application papers to another college returned because the college wanted to avoid showing on its records that a Parsons student had even applied. Parsons students were met with guffaws from other students when they gave the name of their institution.

All this served ultimately to unify rather than divide both the faculty and the student body. Because of its problems rather than in spite of them, the college found a new spirit developing in 1968 and 1969 and a certain loyalty that had not been much in evidence before. There was general frustration, and some bitterness, at the failure to gain reaccreditation in those years but it was tempered by "adversity's sweet milk, philosophy" and perhaps by the confidence that reaccreditation would come in time.

NCA sent another visiting team to the college in 1968 and will do so yet again in 1970. The 1968 team had reservations about Parsons's ability to meet its financial problems but wrote a favorable report and recommended to NCA that the full accreditation of Parsons be restored. Once again, however, the NCA executive board, as it had done in 1967, vetoed the recommendations of its own examiners and refused to reaccredit. But it did grant Parsons the status of Recognized Candidate for Accreditation, implying that it expected to reaccredit Parsons in the future but did not have enough faith in the college at the time. Parsons sympathizers would doubtless hold that it was not a matter of NCA's faith but of its determination to punish Parsons for its past by keeping it in exile for a while longer.

By May of 1969 Parsons had completed still another full-dress self-study of the kind required by NCA in preparation for a visit. NCA and the other regional accrediting associations make a great deal of these self-studies, claiming that they are invaluable for the institution itself. If so, Parsons, having conducted five complete self-evaluations in about eleven years (and having been through six complete assessments by NCA) is surely one of the most introspective colleges in the country; whatever virtues inhere in NCA self-studies Parsons must have in great abundance, though mixed perhaps with some neuroticism from such prolonged contemplation of self.

Since Roberts's departure, Parsons has striven to refine the most promising elements of the Parsons Plan and to jettison the rest. One of the first changes was to greatly strengthen the authority of the faculty. Because of its increased power, the faculty now might be able to mold Parsons into the kind of genuinely experimental school that Roberts claimed it was. The Parsons Plan might now be given a real trial at the new Parsons. A strong commitment continues to the tightly controlled curriculum, but with some loosening up in the core courses and with some additions to the upper-division offerings. There has been additional emphasis on the accessibility of faculty members to students and on personal counseling, which has now become a major facet of life at Parsons, one that distinguishes it from the majority of American institutions. And there is at last a retention policy that does not allow a student to stay on indefinitely, even though the college now needs students more than at any time since 1955. The summer trimester has been split into two segments in order to have more appeal to students than the old single-block summer, and a new remedial program has been introduced in the summer to prepare weak students for the regular fall trimester.

But all these are tentative gropings. The main fact is that Parsons's principal concern for the time being must be survival. There are those, including Roberts himself, who doubt that the college can survive with academics rather than

Roberts running the show. My own bet is that it will survive, will recover its accreditation in 1970, will grow slowly for some years, and in time might become an experimental institution of some note. At the moment it seems to be striding pretty firmly along the road back to respectability which, memories of the old Parsons being what they are among educators, may not turn out to be a short journey.

The Lessons of Parsons College

Any further discussion at this point of the lessons of Parsons College must be to some extent an adumbration of the obvious, for the "lessons" are inherent in the story itself and I have already pointed to many of them. Yet I would not like to close this tale without at least a glance at what Parsons might have been and at what other colleges might take away from the Parsons experience.

Parsons might have been a far-reaching experiment in educational economics that would have been hard even for its natural enemies to ignore. It might have been a unique exploration in ways to educate college drop-outs and low-ability students, a tormented problem that is going to get worse in the United States and possibly throughout the world. It might have been an effort to solve a problem everybody talks about but nobody tackles: how to train college teachers to teach well— the Parsons system of team teaching might have been made into a supervised apprenticeship of a kind that has not been tried. It might have been an experiment in the financial, logistical, and educational advantages of an affiliated group of colleges. In view of the paucity of knowledge about such matters, what Parsons might have been represents a challenge to the new Parsons as well as a challenge perhaps to some other institutions.

Certainly one lesson comes through clearly and bears re-iteration: the self-perpetuating board of trustees that prevails among our private colleges, that is dominated by noneducators and answerable to nobody, needs reassessment. The Parsons record is a strong reinforcement of the view that such boards, however well meaning, may be dangerously remote from both the professional and the public interest that they presumably represent. I would not hold, as many people would, that they are anachronistic or that they should be replaced with a differ-ent piece of governing machinery, but Parsons affords a splendid illustration of the trustee problem, as described recently by an experienced administrator:

Most educators have seen what happens when a board, year after year, passively follows a president. All too often, soft spots are covered up, festering crises glossed over, and administrative ineptitude artfully concealed. Disturbing trends are ignored simply because the board hears only what it wants to hear.[3]

The Parsons board followed Roberts passively far too long and seemed impervious to warnings. After the Parsons bubble had burst, one member of the board of trustees appeared before the faculty to say that he for the first time had really discovered what had been going on and that if the faculty were to ask him why he had not known before, he could offer only a very unsatisfactory answer. One reason the trustees did not know as much as they should have was the failure of NCA to tell them in so many words that action was needed. In all of the NCA reports, there is scarcely a mention of the board of trustees and when there is, as in the 1959 report, it is to praise them, not to inform or nudge them.

Of course, the way in which trustees are chosen has some-thing to do with the problem. They are not expected, as Algo

Henderson observes, to be troublemakers on the board, but to be donors and supporters of the administration:

> . . . board members too often are selected for their ability to make gifts. . . . Much as the money is needed, the policy seems unwise. It puts into the hands of persons chosen by a single criterion the governance of institutions in which there is a substantial public interest. Our colleges and universities deserve to be governed by persons who have been selected on grounds other than sheer expediency.[4]

That expediency has a lot to do with selection is also supported by a recent study in which no fewer than 5,000 trustees returned questionnaires about their own backgrounds:

> In general, trustees are male, in their 50's (though, nationally more than a third are over 60), white (fewer than two percent in our sample are Negro), well-educated, and financially well-off (more than half have annual incomes exceeding $30,000). They occupy prestige occupations, frequently in medicine, law and education, but more often as business executives (in the total sample over 35 per cent are executives of manufacturing, merchandising or investment firms and at private universities nearly 50 per cent hold such positions). As a group, then, they personify "success" in the usual American sense of that word.[5]

The explanation usually offered for the failures of the Parsons trustees is that Roberts dazzled and overwhelmed them with his reports and graphs, entertained them in diverting places like Fort Lauderdale, carefully shielded them from Parsons's critics, and got rid of any trustee who gave him trouble. Wayne Stamper, Parsons's second acting president after the departure of Roberts, wrote of the Roberts era:

Trustees that began to oppose various practices of the President discovered that they were no longer members of the Board or were relegated to committee positions in which they could accomplish little in the policy making function. It is quite evident that the success of the President in achieving certain goals permitted him to gain control of his Board to the extent often desired by college presidents but seldom achieved.[6]

Whatever the reasons, the Parsons board consistently supported Roberts's "commercial" approach to education with his talk about profits, cost accounting, and the application of business principles to Parsons. And yet there were many warnings that went unheeded by the trustees. As early as 1960 they had in hand the special committee report of the church which invited them to take corrective action and offered them help. They had successive reports of the Board of Visitors of the church. They had The Dissident Report in 1963 which, had they acted on it even to the extent of an informal inquiry, might well have avoided future trouble—it was, after all, the failure of the trustees to act on that document that caused the dissidents to send their report to NCA, thereby forging the first link in the chain with which NCA ultimately shackled the college. They had other kinds of warnings from many quarters. But they were busy people; they were misinformed; and they were too inclined to give their flamboyant president his head.

The Parsons board now is much more effective, having learned a great many lessons. It has distributed power to the faculty and instituted tight financial controls on the administration. It has made provision for hearing directly from both the faculty and the student body and has put many other reforms into effect. The Parsons board, in a word, has learned its business the hard way. Whatever reforms may be needed generally in the governance of college and universities, other trustees could do a lot worse than consider the experience of the Parsons College board; it has much to teach them.

Parsons offers other lessons too. Take, for example, the question of "profit" in higher education. Nothing could illustrate better the dominance of opinion over evidence in regard to this abrasive question than the suit of Marjorie Webster Junior College against the Middle States Association. Although Roberts gave the idea of profit an even worse reputation than it would normally have in education, that lawsuit is a lengthy testament to both the ignorance and prejudice of educators on the point, and to their inflexibility and unwillingness to substitute experiment for dogma. Without worrying the problem here, I would simply suggest that American education needs all the options and alternatives it can find and cannot afford to make negative *a priori* judgments about the possible contribution of profit-making institutions to our system of higher education. On the contrary, we ought to be anxious to give such institutions a trial. If they can offer a service that people are willing to pay for and can make a profit and pay taxes while supplying that service, perhaps they should have our blessing and perhaps the nonprofit institutions might themselves learn something from them.

Or take the problem of how to maintain even a dual, not to say a pluralistic, system of private and public institutions. All the supply-demand projections available in higher education suggest that a very difficult time lies ahead for private institutions, but most of these institutions do not seem to be engaging in any central or long-range planning to insure their survival. Instead of overhauling their managerial practices and educational controls to achieve an increased efficiency, they seem to be either oblivious to the future or ready to throw in the towel and "go public" as the easiest way out. None of the five universities, according to one researcher, which have

gone public in recent years confessed to being forced to do so
through any lack of foresight or to any internal mismanagement on their own part, though there was in fact a great deal
of both.[7] Instead of creating distinctive programs of their
own that would offer students an option outside the tax-supported system, they try to compete with the public colleges on
the public colleges' own terms.

Yet the Parsons experience indicates that a college that
will map out its own territory and offer something not readily
available in public institutions can survive and prosper. Not
everybody would care for Parsons's territory or would want
to make the rehabilitation of problem students their special
concern. But some private colleges may not have a choice, for
the acceptance of increasing numbers of average and below-
average students may represent their only chance of survival.
The simple fact is that the growth in college enrollments is
coming mostly from these groups of students, not from the
ranks of high-ability students. The numbers of talented students able to pay private tuition fees, and willing to do so
instead of going to a public institution, are smaller than many
people realize and such students are in any case apt to go to
a relatively small group of prestige schools.[8]

We are now as a nation reaching well down into the high
school population and the IQ range for the greatest part of
the enrollment increase in colleges. Without arguing here the
wisdom or folly of this movement, I would say simply that
we ought to recognize that the movement is probably permanent and that the colleges are not prepared to deal with it.
The reason they are not prepared to deal with it is that, with
the exception of Parsons, they have not undertaken to experiment seriously and on the required scale with the education of
such students. One can quarrel with the attempt made by
Parsons, but at least a body of experience exists there that
other colleges could look at, relating not only to the problem

of educating low-ability students but that of educating drop-outs (which is not always the same problem) from other colleges.

Or if we consider any of the other elements of the Parsons Plan, we have to confess a similar state of ignorance. What do educators really know about class size and its relationship to learning? Only that some large classes work and a lot of small ones don't. What do educators really know about the effects of a sharply restricted curriculum, especially for below-average students? Only that it seems to work at least as well as the smorgasbord curriculum characteristic of American colleges and that it is much cheaper. What do educators really know about training people for college and university teaching? Only that nobody has made an attack on the problem sufficient to discover what might work. As Jacques Barzun has remarked, college teaching is "the only profession (except the proverbially oldest in the world) for which no training is given or required. It is supposed to be 'picked up.' "[9] What do educators know about faculty "productivity" and whether professors can be expected to pay their way? Only that it is an issue that needs to be explored.

Parsons's experience on all these points is at least worth a serious examination. Even though many institutions would reject the open-door, second-chance philosophy of Parsons, and would certainly not admire the college's methods of carrying that philosophy out, they might still be well-advised to forget their prejudices against Parsons and see if there is not something, after all, that they can learn from the rise and fall of Parsons College. I have particularly in mind, of course, private colleges that are in financial straits. And their name is Legion.

N O T E S

[1] James Ridgeway, *The Closed Corporation: American Universities in Crisis* (New York: Random House, 1968).

[2] Paul Woodring, *The Higher Learning in America: A Reassessment* (New York: McGraw-Hill, 1968), p. 14.

[3] Ernest L. Boyer, "A Fresh Look at the College Trustee," *Educational Record* (Summer, 1968), p. 277.

[4] "The Role of the Governing Board," Association of Governing Boards of Universities and Colleges (October, 1967).

[5] Rodney T. Hartnett, "College and University Trustees" (Princeton: Educational Testing Service, 1969), p. 19.

[6] Parsons's *Institutional Profile* (1968).

[7] John Oliver Hall, "Will Private Universities Survive? A Study of Five that Did Not" (doctoral dissertation, University of Pittsburgh, 1968).

[8] See Humphrey Doermann, *Crosscurrents in College Admissions* (New York: Teachers College Press, 1968), p. 6.

[9] Jacques Barzun, *The American University: How It Runs, Where It Is Going* (New York: Harper & Row, 1968), p. 36.

Index